# PROCLAMATION

# EASTER

**INTERPRETING
THE LESSONS OF
THE CHURCH YEAR**

**JAMES LIMBURG**

**PROCLAMATION 5
SERIES B**

FORTRESS PRESS   MINNEAPOLIS

PROCLAMATION 5
Interpreting the Lessons of the Church Year
Series B, Easter

Cover and interior design: Spangler Design Team

Library of Congress Cataloging-in-Publication Data available

ISBN 0-8006-4189-2

The paper used in this publication meets the minimum requirements of American National Standard for Information Sciences—Permanence of Paper for Printed Library Materials, ANSI Z329.48-1984. ∞™

Manufactured in the U.S.A.                                                           AF 1-4189
98     97     96     95     94     1     2     3     4     5     6     7     8     9     10

# CONTENTS

# The Resurrection of Our Lord
# Easter Day

| Lutheran | Roman Catholic | Episcopal | Common Lectionary |
|---|---|---|---|
| Isa. 25:6-9 | Acts 10:34a, 37-43 | Acts 10:34-43 | Acts 10:34-43 or Isa. 25:6-9 |
| 1 Cor. 15:19-28 | Col. 3:1-4 | Col. 3:1-4 | 1 Cor. 15:1-11 or Acts 10:34-43 |
| Mark 16:1-8 | John 20:1-9 | Mark 16:1-8 | John 20:1-18 or Mark 16:1-8 |

These readings for Easter get right to the heart of things. They deal with matters of life and death—or better stated, matters of death and life. At the center of the Isaiah text is the promise that one day the Lord "will swallow up death forever" (Isa. 25:7). Paul writes to the Corinthians that "the last enemy to be destroyed is death" (1 Cor. 15:26). The young man sitting in the tomb tells the three women, "He has been raised; he is not here" (Mark 16:6). Each of these texts speaks about death, and about life.

## NO MORE DEATH
## ISAIAH 25:6-9

Isaiah 24–27 has often been called the "Isaiah Apocalypse" because some themes typical of apocalyptic writings such as Daniel and Revelation are found here. We hear of universal destruction (24:1-3), cosmic upheaval (24:4), and the end of death and sorrow (25:7-8). These prophetic words stretch our imagination in two directions. First, they paint a series of seven pictures of God's final acts in the far-distant future, each introduced with "on that day" (24:21; 25:9; 26:1; 27:1, 2, 12, 13). Second, their focus is neither on Judah (Isaiah 1–12), nor even on the great nations of the time (Isaiah 13–23), but rather on the whole earth (e.g., 24:1, 3, 4, 5).

There are no clues for dating these materials. Probably the most that can be said is that we have here a collection of pieces gathered at the time of the final editing of the Isaiah book, sometime in the postexilic period.

The assigned text divides into two parts. Isaiah 25:6-8 is a prophetic saying, ending with the formula "for the LORD has spoken." With 25:9 a second "on that day" introduces a short hymn, continuing through 10a.

Verse 6 describes a great banquet in the future. "This mountain" is a reference to Mount Zion (24:23). The Lord is pictured here as the host at the banquet. The image is a familiar one in the Bible; one thinks of Ps. 23:5-6 or of the banquet scenes in the parables of Jesus (Matt. 22:1-14). This is no exclusive party for insiders; present will be "all peoples." And what will be served? "Rich food" (see also 28:1, 4) has the literal sense of food that is loaded with goodness. The wines are well-aged, and therefore the best.

Verse 7 sets before us images of death. The custom at mourning was to cover oneself with black garments, to indicate sadness. In this prophetic vision all peoples (the same as in v. 6) are covered with this mourning garment. The parallel statement says the same thing. The whole world is covered with sadness, suffering, and mourning.

And now comes the good news: The shroud draped over the world will be destroyed. The Lord will "swallow up" death. The word is the same as that for Jonah being swallowed by the great fish (Jon. 1:17) or for a person gulping down the first ripe fig of the season (Isa. 28:4). So quickly, completely, and permanently will death be destroyed!

Verse 8 indicates not only will death be swallowed up, but tears will be taken away and God's people will no longer suffer disgrace. The expression "for the LORD has spoken" certifies the prophecy.

In vv. 9-10a, "on that day" introduces a short hymn that focuses on the distant future, when all the longing and waiting will be past and joy and gladness are finally present. "This mountain" in v. 10 picks up the same phrase from v. 6, tying the whole section together.

In sum, there are two pictures here. First is the picture of the great banquet, with the finest food and the best wine. All are invited. Jesus speaks about such a banquet, when many will come from east and west (Luke 13:29). The celebration of the Lord's Supper anticipates that banquet (Matt. 26:29; see also Luke 14:15-24 and Rev. 19:9). Second is the picture of the defeat of death. On that future day, the Lord will swallow up the shroud of death that has been hanging over the nations of the earth. More than that, death itself will be destroyed, and every tear will be wiped away! The same imagery occurs in Rev. 7:17 and 21:4, where the writer sees the new heaven and new earth.

When will this defeat of death begin? The next texts deal with that question.

## SO WHAT ABOUT DEATH?
## 1 CORINTHIANS 15:19-28

If you think you've got problems in your congregation, give Paul's letters to the Corinthians another reading! Paul himself had worked in Corinth (Acts 18). Now he is across the Aegean at Ephesus (16:8) as he writes this letter, sometime in the early 50s, A.D. He has heard about some of the problems in Corinth through a letter they had written (7:1, 25; 8:1; 12:1; 16:1, 12). Other matters came to his attention by word of mouth (15:12).

After the traditional opening (1:1-9), the apostle gives some pastoral advice, dealing with matters of unity (chaps. 1–4), sexuality (5–7), Christian freedom (8–10), worship (11–14), death (15), and (typical preacher, some might have said) the offering (16). On this Easter Sunday, our concern is with what Paul says about death—or better, about death and life.

In order to understand chap. 15, we begin with v. 12, where the problem Paul is addressing comes into sharp focus. The Good News Bible puts it, "how can some of you say that the dead will not be raised to life?" Where did these new Christians in Corinth pick up that notion? Were some saying that the soul will live on but the body will not be raised? Or were they saying, "when you're dead, you're dead, and that's it"? We do not know. What we do know is that they were touching on something right at the heart of Paul's preaching of the good news. Did he save this issue until (almost) last in his letter because of its importance?

Paul begins by saying: Let me remind you of the good news that I preached to you not long ago (15:1-11). In the first couple of verses the Greek word *evangelion*—"good news"—or its related verb form comes up three times: "I remind you of the *evangel* with which I *evangelized* you, which you received, in which you stand, through which you are being saved, through which word I *evangelized* you." In vv. 3-11, Paul summarizes the heart of his preaching: (1) Christ died for our sins in accordance with what the Old Testament promised; (2) Christ was buried; (3) Christ was raised, in accordance with the Old Testament; (4) Christ appeared to Cephas (Peter), the Twelve, and hundreds more. "So we preached," says Paul, "and so you believed. At the center of our preaching is the good news that Jesus Christ was raised from the dead."

Then Paul grants his opponents their position and follows that position out to its logical consequences (vv. 12-19). If there is no resurrection, then: (*a*) Christ has not been raised; (*b*) our preaching has been a waste of time; (c) your believing has also been for nothing. Paul goes through the argument once again, saying that if the dead are not raised, then: (*a*) Christ has not been raised; (*b*) your faith is futile; (*c*) you are still in your sins; (*d*) those who have died are lost forever. "If our hope is only for this life, then we are to be pitied!" he concludes.

Paul winds up by taking a positive tack, preaching the good news straight from the shoulder. "But in fact Christ has been raised from the dead. . . ." He uses a picture drawn from the life of a farmer: the risen Christ is the "first fruits" (Exod. 23:19; Lev. 23:10; Deut. 26:1-11). When a farmer brings in the first of the crop and shows it happily to his family, this is an indication that (1) there will be more to come, and (2) there will be more of the same kind to come. If Christ's resurrection is the first fruits, this means that there will be more resurrections, and that they will be similar to this one.

Later on, Paul will speak about the kind of body believers will have in heaven (vv. 35-58). Note his initial answer to the question raised in v. 35, "You foolish person!" (NRSV, "Fool!"). As Reinhold Niebuhr once said, God has not chosen to describe for us in detail either the furniture of heaven or the temperature of hell! But Paul does say something about the individual's resurrection life in this section, stressing both the dimensions of sameness and difference, speaking of identity without being identical.

Paul sets up the parallel between Adam and Christ in vv. 21-22. The best commentary on these verses is found in Handel's *Messiah*. The composer begins in a minor key, "Since by man came death" (see the KJV), and then shifts abruptly to a major, "by man came also the resurrection of the dead." The same musical theme is repeated for v. 22.

The segment ends as Paul picks up a couple of quotations from the Old Testament, citing today's Isaiah text (25:7) in v. 26, and playing upon Ps. 8:6 in vv. 27-28.

In sum: Some in the congregation at Corinth were saying that there was no hope for life after death. The way in which Paul deals with this problem is a model of pastoral care: He argues from the center, the good news, addressing that gospel to the real-life problem at hand.

## LET LOOSE IN THE WORLD
## MARK 16:1-8

The first thing we notice in reading Mark's version of these events is the confusion about where the story stops. After v. 8, the NRSV goes on to provide an additional "shorter ending" as well as the traditional "longer ending," known from the King James Version. The fact of the matter is, however, that the best Greek manuscripts, including Sinaiticus and Vaticanus, end Mark's Gospel with v. 8. Whether we like it or not, there can be little doubt that this is where the original Gospel ended. Early on, there were those who did not like this ending and who made additions to it. It does seem a strange way to end an account of "good news," with three women running from a tomb, terrified. Can one make sense out of a story that concludes in this way?

In the manner of a television serial reviewing its previous episode, let us begin by looking in on the events described at the close of Mark 15. It is Friday evening. A number of women are standing in a group, looking toward three crosses on a hill. Mary Magdalene, Mary the mother of James and Joses, Salome, and some other women had followed Jesus when he was in far-off Galilee (15:40-41).

We next see Joseph of Arimathea, a respected member of the Jewish community. He takes matters into his own hands and asks Pilate for the body of Jesus. He wants to give Jesus a proper Jewish burial, and he does so. He puts the body in a tomb in a rocky hillside and rolls the stone in front of it to close it up. Visitors to Jerusalem today will be shown a tomb from that period, the stone a heavy disk made to roll in a track in front of the opening (15:42-47).

Saturday, the Sabbath, finally comes to an end. Again, the story focuses on those three women. They had been with Jesus when he was in the midst of his life's work, teaching, preaching, healing up north in Galilee (15:41). Now these three will be with him at the end, as they go to carry out the traditional rite of anointing the body with pleasant-smelling spices (the Greek word for spices is *arōma*; see also Luke 23:56 and John 19:40).

The women waited until the Sabbath was over. The story emphasizes that they went early: "very early . . . when the sun had risen." Little did these three realize, when they got up so early on that first Easter Sunday, that they would establish an early-rising tradition that would be followed by Christians all over the world for centuries!

The women knew that they were not strong enough to push that stone down its track. But now, with v. 4, the surprises begin. The stone—and here is emphasized what a huge and heavy one it was—had been rolled away from the opening to the tomb. They walk into the tomb and see "a young man, dressed in a white robe"; the other Gospels will identify him as an angel (Matthew) or remember that there were two persons there (Luke).

In this account, the focus is still on the women. Their reaction? They are alarmed, amazed, astonished; one thinks of them stepping back, eyes wide open, hands over their mouths.

And now, in the midst of this place of death, comes a word about life. First, there is a pastoral word, directed toward the perplexed women: "Do not be alarmed." Then the Greek text names the one they were looking for: "Jesus you are seeking—the Nazarene—the one who has been crucified." Finally there is a word about life, announced here in this place of death. "He has been raised; he is not here." Then, to confirm this astonishing announcement, the young man points to the place where Jesus had been lying, "Look, there is the place. . . ."

On previous occasions Jesus had asked that the word about what he was doing (Mark 1:44) or who he was (8:30; 9:9) not be spread. Now, however, the secret is out. The lid is open. The young man commissions this trio as history's first Christian missionaries: "Go, tell!" With this is the promise that "you will see him [in Galilee], just as he told you" (14:28).

And now comes the puzzling part. We might expect the women to run down the road, shouting for joy, telling the world what they had seen. But the story says that they went out, running away from the tomb, shaking with fear (that is the sense of the Greek behind *terror*) and beside themselves (the literal sense of the Greek). The women run away. They are silent and afraid. And so Mark's version of the story ends.

If we are disappointed with this sort of ending to such a story, we are not the first. Others were not comfortable with Mark's ending—and added something about later appearances and the proclaiming of the good news and miracles being performed (vv. 9-20).

Why would Mark end the story as he does? Is this an indication that humans, even those closest to Jesus, often are not heroes but remain human? Is it a reminder that the real power behind the good news is the power of God, which can accomplish what God wills even without our help? Is it a reminder of the enormity of this event, which could be initially encountered only with a reaction of fear and trembling, of terror and silence? Was this bringing of life out of death an event of such power that one could not immediately begin to talk about it? Such questions this strange ending invites us to ponder.

I conclude with a story that I once heard, told by a theologian from Germany. He spoke about life in Soviet Russia, when the Communists were in control and in their heyday. A young soldier, an enthusiastic Marxist, came upon a group of people in a little village who had gathered to remember Easter. The soldier reminded them that such gatherings were not allowed. He went on to praise communism, the new savior, and to ridicule Christianity, and especially the absurd belief in Christ's resurrection. When he finished, a voice from the rear of the crowd spoke the words from the Russian Easter liturgy: "Christ is risen!" As if they were assembled in a service in a great cathedral, the response of those gathered was automatic and instantaneous: "He is risen indeed!"

The good news, first announced by that young man in a tomb, has been let loose in the world.

# Easter Evening or
# Easter Monday

| Lutheran | Roman Catholic | Episcopal | Common Lectionary |
|---|---|---|---|
| Dan. 12:1c-3 *or* Jon. 2:2-9 | Acts 2:14, 22-32 | Acts 5:29a, 30-32 *or* Dan. 12:1-3 | Acts 5:29-32 *or* Dan. 12:1-3 |
| 1 Cor. 5:6-8 | | 1 Cor. 5:6b-8 *or* Acts 5:29a, 30-32 | 1 Cor. 5:6-8 *or* Acts 5:29-32 |
| Luke 24:13-49 | Matt. 26:8-15 | Luke 24:13-35 | Luke 24:13-49 |

The texts for this time just after the main Easter service offer opportunities to preach sermons that go in three differing directions, each flowing out of the Easter events.

## THEY ARE PRECIOUS IN HIS SIGHT
## JONAH 2:2-9

While the lectionary focuses only on Jonah's prayer from the belly of the fish (see Matt. 12:40), that prayer should be put in context by retelling the story of Jonah.

*1:1-3.* Jonah did not want to accept the assignment to Nineveh because Nineveh was a great Assyrian city and the Assyrians were remembered as among the worst of Israel's enemies. In 722 B.C. they destroyed Samaria and deported the inhabitants (2 Kings 17). The prophet Nahum predicted the fall of Nineveh, which took place in 612 B.C. One need only read through sections of that book to get a sense of the hatred of that Assyrian city (Nahum 3, for example). Carry out a mission to Nineveh? No way, said Jonah. He set out for far-away Spain (Tarshish) instead.

*1:4-16.* Observe the actions of the people of the world (the sailors) in contrast to the actions of the representative of the people of God (Jonah). When the storm hits, the sailors are out praying and working; Jonah is down in the hold, asleep. The captain, again a non-Israelite, awakens Jonah and calls upon him—to pray! When Jonah tells the sailors to throw him overboard in order to save their own necks, they risk their lives, struggling to get the ship back to shore. Finally they do throw him into the sea, the storm stops, and the sailors give thanks and become worshipers of the God of Israel. Given half a chance, these sailors become believers and worshipers of the true God. Jonah has been a successful missionary, in spite of himself.

*1:17—2:10.* The story continues by telling that Jonah was swallowed by a huge fish in which he spent three days, and was eventually spit out of the fish (1:17; 2:10). These narrative statements frame the prayer that is the assigned text for this day. Notice that the prayer is a true prayer, addressing God as "you" (2b-6, 7b, 9a) but that it also speaks *about* the Lord, in the third person (2a, 7a, 9b). These third-person sections indicate that this prayer is intended to be a witness to others, telling them what the Lord did for Jonah. The implication is clear: If the Lord rescued Jonah, the Lord can also rescue you.

*3, 4.* The Lord gives Jonah a second chance. His short speech in Nineveh hits the Assyrians like a match setting off an explosion. The whole city repents and God calls off the announced punishment. Once more the people of the world are the good people in this story! Note that the animals repent, too (3:8), and that God cares about them (4:11). This detail indicates a sense of solidarity among all creatures that sounds quite modern in this time of new ecological awareness.

We might expect that a prophet would be overjoyed at such a positive reaction to his preaching. Jonah, however, sulks and is angry. He can quote the catechism with accuracy (4:2; see also Exod. 34:6-7). But there is something wrong with his attitude toward the people of the world. He cannot bear to think of them worshiping the same God that he worships. He would rather be dead than to see these people as members of his church (4:1-3).

The story concludes with the Lord giving the prophet some instruction, and thereby instructing all of us who read or hear the story. The Lord asks Jonah a question. "You are very concerned about what happens to one bush, which has been around only for a day and a night. Don't you think that I am concerned about what happens to one of the great cities of the world? Don't you think I care about its people—and even the animals that live there?"

And so the story ends. What could it mean for us today, specifically for Christians in this Easter season? First, Jonah clearly had a problem with his attitude toward his non-Israelite neighbors, the Assyrians. We ought to ask ourselves: Do we know what it is to harbor prejudice against those who are not part of our immediate group? This story says that God cares about the people of the far-off cities of the world. That old Sunday school song had it right: "Red and yellow, black and white, they are precious in his sight, Jesus loves the little children of the world."

Second, this story says that God cares about the people of Nineveh, even about the cows grazing on the Assyrian hillsides. The story uses the familiar "how much more" argumentation of the Bible (Deut. 31:27; 2 Kings 5:13; Matt. 6:30). If God cares about Assyrian cattle, I ought to know that God also cares about me. Jesus said somewhat the same thing, though he spoke about the sparrows in the city of Jerusalem (Matt. 10:29-31). Finally, Jonah is a book that sets before us the missionary calling of the people of God. Jonah is the only prophet in the Old Testament pictured as walking down the streets of a city outside of Israel and proclaiming the Lord's message there. Jonah is there because God cares even about Nineveh, that great—but wicked—city. Jesus has made clear that God loves all the people of the world (John 3:16) and has made clear the obligation of Christian people to get that word out, through preaching, baptizing, and teaching (Matt. 28:16-20).

## WHAT'S NEW?
## 1 CORINTHIANS 5:6-8

How should we understand the death and resurrection of Jesus Christ? This was the question for the church's first preachers and teachers, and it remains a question for us today. In this short segment of Paul's letter to the young church at Corinth, he provides us with one of his answers.

Paul is writing to a congregation that had plenty of problems; see the discussion in connection with 1 Corinthians 15 in the previous chapter.

In chaps. 5–7, Paul is dealing with a number of questions in the area of sexuality. For starters, there is the case of a man living with his stepmother (5:1). Our text for this time immediately after the celebration of Easter is situated in the midst of this discussion.

Paul had noted an attitude of pride or arrogance in this young congregation (5:2). Such an attitude is not in order, he says (5:6). He continues with allusions to the celebration of the Passover. In order to understand these allusions, we refer to the directions for that celebration as found in Exodus 12.

This Exodus account tells of the first "passover," that is, the time when the angel of death "passed over" the houses of the Israelites (12:13, 23), but also provides directions for later celebrations remembering this event. Each family is to slaughter a lamb for a meal and put some blood on the doorposts, to identify the home as one where Israelites live. Only unleavened bread is to be eaten, and no leaven is to be found in the house (12:19-20). Bitter herbs are to be eaten (12:8-9). When the meal is eaten in later times, it should be eaten in haste, with the people prepared to be on their way, as a reminder of the way in which that first Passover was celebrated (12:11). When the meal is celebrated this way, the children will ask, "Why are we doing these things?" The parents then have the opportunity to tell the story of what God did when God delivered the Israelites from Egypt.

The observation of Passover or, as it is called in Hebrew, Pesach, continues to be one of the central celebrations for Jewish people today. The celebration takes place at home, in the circle of the family. One of the important practices associated with the celebration is cleaning the house of any hametz or leaven; this is a ritual associated with spring cleaning, and involves the hiding of bits of leaven in the house. "Bitter herbs" in the form of horseradish are eaten, as a reminder of the bitterness of captivity in Egypt. A portion of lamb is on the menu. (For further discussion of the connections between Passover and

Easter, see J. Limburg, ed., *Judaism: An Introduction for Christians* [Augsburg, 1987], 102–5.)

Against this background of the celebration of Passover, Paul gives some practical advice on how to deal with the case of sexual immorality. A little yeast makes the whole loaf of bread rise, he says. In the same way, one such instance of immorality can affect the whole congregation. So, says Paul, the immoral person should be dismissed from the church, so that his actions do not have a bad effect on the whole community (5:13).

Then, still working against this Passover background, Paul provides a new picture to help understand what happened on Good Friday and Easter. Just as the Passover lamb, when sacrificed, brought deliverance for the community in Egypt, so now the sacrifice of Christ has brought deliverance for the new community, the Christian church. The picture of Christ as Passover Lamb was used by other New Testament writers as well (1 Pet. 1:19; John 1:29, 36; Rev. 5:6, 9, 12; 12:11). Finally, Paul plays again on this Passover imagery. After the sacrifice is over, the time to celebrate has come. Christ, the new Passover Lamb, has been sacrificed and now, says Paul, let us celebrate! Let us get rid of the "old yeast" of malice and evil, and instead let our congregation be like the "unleavened bread" of sincerity and truth.

This short text makes a number of important contributions during this Easter season. First, it gives us a fresh picture of the work of Christ. Christ has accomplished a new exodus, not from the bondage of Egypt but from the bondage of sin and death. This means that the central message of the Christian faith, the death and resurrection of Jesus Christ, is to be understood in terms of imagery taken from the Old Testament and Judaism.

Second, these words from Paul remind us of the link between the faith of the Old Testament and that of the New. When Paul wants to describe the Christ event, he uses imagery drawn from the Old Testament and the practices of the Jewish community. Finally, this text can give occasion to reflect on the relationships between Christians and Jews. Sadly, it was at Easter time that many Christians traditionally carried out acts of hostility against Jews. Jewish friends have told me that as children, they were afraid to be out on the streets at Easter time, for fear of being beaten up by "Christian" playmates. This text could provide an occasion for pointing out how the New Testament is linked to the Old, and how the Christian church has its roots in Judaism. Instead of an occasion for intensified anti-Jewish actions, Easter could become a time for Christian and Jewish communities to learn about one another. (For further help, see J. Limburg, ed., *Judaism: An Introduction for Christians*.)

## WHAT WILL KEEP US GOING?
## LUKE 24:13-49

This Lukan text is a natural for a service on Easter evening, since that is the setting for the stories that the text tells. Everything takes place "on that same day" on the road to Emmaus (v. 13), near the end of that day in an Emmaus hotel (v. 29), and back in Jerusalem in the evening (v. 33). These are some of Luke's finest stories and are effective as they are simply retold. The text divides into the account of Jesus' appearance on the road to Emmaus (vv. 13-35), and an account of an appearance in Jerusalem (vv. 36-49). Because this second appearance is the Gospel text for the Third Sunday of Easter, we shall focus on vv. 13-35 here and work with vv. 36-49 in connection with that later Sunday. The preacher wishing to deal with both stories in one sermon can combine these comments with those for the Third Sunday of Easter.

The fact that both of these accounts are so explicitly tied to the first Easter Sunday suggests that from earliest times, the texts were used on that day. They deal with themes of central importance to the early church and to the church throughout its history: Scripture and Lord's Supper, Word and Sacrament.

The first scene in the Emmaus account takes place while two people are walking along a road; its focus is on words (vv. 13-27). The second scene takes place in a restaurant; its focus is on an act (vv. 28-35).

*13-27.* Two of those who believed in Jesus are taking a Sunday walk on the road from Jerusalem to Emmaus. One is named Cleopas; the other remains unnamed. As the story is told, it is suggested that God himself is controlling these events. When these two first meet Jesus, "their eyes were kept from recognizing him" (16). As they sat with Jesus at supper, "their eyes were opened" (31).

*17-24.* The conversation gets going when this "stranger" (18) raises a question (17); the scene in Jerusalem proceeds in the same way (38). The stranger pretends not to know about what has been happening in the city. This gives occasion for these two to tell the story of the life and death of Jesus. They had hoped that this Jesus would be the one to "redeem" the people of Israel; the Greek word can be used to denote Israel's deliverance from a potential military disaster (1 Macc. 4:11; Sir. 48:20) or also Christ's deliverance from sin (Titus 2:14). Early on in Luke's story, two faithful senior citizens announced the deliverance that Jesus would bring about using this same word (Zechariah in Luke 1:68; Anna in Luke 2:38).

*25-27.* All of this gives Jesus occasion to conduct an on-the-road Bible study, aimed at showing that the long-awaited Messiah would have to suffer. Verse 26 says that it was necessary that these things happen; we are to understand that this necessity was part of God's plan, as is also the case when this expression is used in Acts 1:16; 17:3; and Luke 4:43.

*28-35.* Even after this biblical instruction, these two did not know the identity of the stranger with whom they had been walking. They did, however, remember to show hospitality to strangers (Genesis 18; Heb. 13:2) and invited him to join them for supper and lodging. As they sat at table, something astonishing happened. As the event is described, the language is that of the institution of the Lord's Supper (Luke 22:19; cf. 9:16). In these actions, these two travelers recognize that it is Jesus who is with them—and then he is suddenly gone. They talk about their experience and recall the powerful effects of that traveling Bible study.

They change their plans. Within an hour, they cancel their hotel reservation and head back to Jerusalem. The eleven disciples who were gathered there on that Easter Sunday evening have a story to tell. Cleopas and his friend have a story, too.

To catch the excitement of this story, we ought to remember that it takes place on that first Easter Sunday. After the crucifixion, the question in the hearts of all of Jesus' followers was How can we keep the faith now? What will keep us going? This story, which Luke surely intended to be retold on each anniversary of that first Easter Sunday, answers the question by saying that the risen Christ has left his believers with two gifts: the Bible, together with a new way of understanding it, and a meal, at which he promised somehow to be present (Luke 22:14-20). The Word and the Sacrament have kept the church going ever since.

# Second Sunday of Easter

| Lutheran | Roman Catholic | Episcopal | Common Lectionary |
|---|---|---|---|
| Acts 3:13-15, 17-26 | Acts 4:32-35 | Acts 3:12a, 13-15, 17-26 | Acts 4:32-35 |
| 1 John 5:1-6 | 1 John 5:1-6 | 1 John 5:1-6 | 1 John 1:1—2:2 |
| John 20:19-31 | John 20:19-31 | John 20:19-31 | John 20:19-31 |

For this Sunday and the next, the Gospel texts are at the center of the stage. They present scenes from the immediate post-Easter period. These Gospel selections will likely be the preaching texts for these two Sundays, with the lessons providing supplementary material.

Each of the lessons for these next eight Sundays includes a selection from Acts. Another possibility, therefore, would be to preach a series of sermons on Acts. Each Sunday except for Pentecost itself also includes a text from 1 John. These weeks provide an opportunity for the preacher to brush up on these two biblical books.

## THIS COULD BE THE START OF SOMETHING BIG
## ACTS 3:13-15, 17-26

This speech of Peter must be put in the context of the story told in Acts 3:1-11; the lectionary has cut out v. 16, which refers to the healing of the lame man. When that man lying in the temple gate asked Peter and John for a handout, they said to him, "in the name of Jesus Christ of Nazareth, stand up and walk." The man immediately started leaping about, praising God and causing something of a commotion. A crowd gathered around Peter and John, which gave Peter the occasion to make the speech that is in today's text.

Because these speeches in the early chapters of Acts present the essentials of early Christian preaching, they are worthy of careful study by both preacher and people. They bring into sharp focus that which is at the center of the Christian faith. The other speeches are found in 2:14-39 (Pentecost); 4:8-12 (Third Sunday of Easter); 5:29-32; 10:34-43; 13:16-41, all addressed to Jewish audiences; and 14:15-17; 17:22-31, addressed to Gentiles.

*11-16.* After the lame man is healed, a crowd gathers. Peter begins by reminding his hearers that they are Israelites—a reminder that is important for understanding what he has to say. These people have a history, a history that can be told by reflecting on their name. Israel was the name given to Jacob, one of the ancestors of those gathered in Jerusalem.

*13.*   The rabbis used to point out that the usual biblical expression is not "the God of Abraham, Isaac, and Jacob," but rather, "the God of Abraham, the God of Isaac, and the God of Jacob" (Exod. 3:6, 15; cf. Luke 20:37). Why should this be? they asked. The answer: So that each generation understands that faith is not inherited. Each generation, each person, must have his or her own relationship to God.

The earliest apostolic preaching typically contains three themes: (1) The promises of the Scriptures are being fulfilled in our days (3:18, 24); (2) the life, death, and resurrection of Jesus represent this fulfillment (3:13-15); and (3) therefore repent, be baptized, and receive forgiveness of sins (3:19).

A good exercise for the Bible student is to go through these speeches in Acts, identifying each of these themes, noting how they are varied and expanded upon, depending on the audience addressed. In so doing, one discovers the good news, the gospel that is at the center of the New Testament and the Christian faith.

*17-26.*   Now the speaker turns to the gathered audience, making the application. Verse 18 speaks of the suffering of the Messiah. Most Jews of the first century thought of the Messiah as a new David, a super-king who would come and put Israel on the political map once again and bring everlasting peace. Taken by themselves, biblical promises like Isaiah 9 and 11 could be understood in this way. Peter, however, says that a careful reading of the Old Testament reveals that the Messiah must suffer, and this picture of a suffering Messiah provides the clue for understanding the person of Jesus.

Note the strong emphasis on the fact that something new is happening these days. The old promises are being fulfilled, right before our eyes (24). These were promises made by the prophets, but also God's promises at the very beginning of Israel's history, when Abraham and Sarah were promised that all families of the earth would be blessed through their descendants.

We conclude with some reflections on this text as a whole:

1. Christianity is not a new religion but rather the fulfillment of an older one. We often speak of Pentecost as "the birthday of the church" and, in a sense, that is so. But as we read the New Testament, we discover that the Christian faith is understood as the completion of the faith of Abraham and Sarah, Isaac and Rebecca, Jacob and Rachel. As we have seen, that faith is not inherited, but comes to each person individually.

2. The Bible is the story of the mighty acts of God. "All of us hear them speaking in our own languages about the great things that God has done!" says Peter in his speech at Pentecost (Acts 2:11, Good News Bible). Notice the subject of the verbs in Peter's speech in Acts 3: God . . . glorified (13) . . . raised (15) . . . fulfilled (18) . . . blesses (25-26). The traditional title of this book is "The Acts of the Apostles." It could also be called "The Acts of God" or of the Holy Spirit.

3. There is a wideness in the good news the speeches announce. This speech is addressed to Jews gathered at the temple in Jerusalem, but it already hints

that the good news of forgiveness and refreshment has wider implications. Peter quoted that ancient promise: "And in your descendants all the families of the earth shall be blessed" (25). The good news comes first to the Jews, but it will not be limited to any one people. These are days when old promises are being fulfilled. But they are also the start of something big.

## KEEPING ON COURSE
## 1 JOHN 5:1-6

The resurrection of Jesus was a unique event. Nothing quite like it has ever happened before or since. The date that you write on every check, or that you find on the corner of your license plate, is a reminder: almost two thousand years ago now, something happened that was so unique that it began a new era. The Bible tells of others who have been raised from the dead (the widow's son, 2 Kings 4; Lazarus, John 11; Jairus's daughter, Mark 5), but all of these died a normal death. The New Testament account of the ascension (Acts 1:1-11) indicates that Jesus did not die such a death.

For those first believers, it took a while for the reality of the resurrection to sink in. The same may be true for us. Easter comes around once again, with bonnets, bunnies, brightly colored eggs, and the beginning of springtime. Those of us who live in northern regions love to feel the sunshine after a long winter and look forward to the summer. And while Easter does have to do with nature, for the Christian it is primarily a celebration of an event that happened in history. Once—and only once—a man died and was raised from death to live again. Events in nature repeat themselves: sunrise and sunset, seedtime and harvest, springtime and fall. Events in history are nonrepeatable: one time you were baptized, one day each of us will die.

The resurrection—a one-time-only event—provides us with a clue to understanding our lives as persons living in nature, but also in history.

Since the events of that first Easter Sunday were so unique, it is not surprising that the New Testament contains all sorts of reflections on that event. The lectionary has already set before us the accounts in Mark 16 and Luke 24. Now, for these next two Sundays, we are directed to focus on John 20 and, again, Luke 24.

Why should the lectionary tradition assign texts from 1 John for the next six Sundays, taking us right up to Pentecost? Before considering the text for this day, we begin with a few observations about that New Testament book.

While we cannot date the three letters of John with precision, scholars are in agreement that they come from a period after the writing of John's Gospel, probably around A.D. 100, and that they come out of the Johannine understanding of the newly forming Christian faith. A careful reading of 1 John indicates that there were some problems in the young church. "Rotten wood doesn't splinter," goes a saying used to justify splinter groups in the modern church; a reading of 1 John indicates that such groups are nothing new. A

18

bit of detective work turns up some clues that tell us something about the division in the young church. One group has separated itself from the mainstream community (2:19). In this group were deceivers (2:26). These people apparently denied that Jesus was the long-awaited Messiah or Christ; the author pulls no punches, calling them liars (2:22). They claim to know Jesus, but their lives are not marked by obedience (1:6; 2:4-6, 9, 11). Reflecting a view current in the time, that "there is something the matter with matter," these deceivers denied that Jesus was truly human. Since they said that he only "seemed" to be human, they were called Docetists, which is Greek for "seemists." This letter counters the Docetic view by saying "We have touched him" (1:1) and that Jesus Christ came "in the flesh" (4:2; also 2 John 7).

We return to our question: Why should the lectionary assign six readings from John for this immediate post-Easter period? The answer is now clear. 1 John is an early reminder that right teaching is important. It is not enough to parrot the old slogan, "Doctrine divides, love unites." No one speaks more about love than the writer of 1 John. But along with this, there is also a passionate concern for getting the teachings about Jesus right.

The text for today includes both of these themes. What it says about Jesus is stated in language that no one could misunderstand: Jesus is the Messiah (Greek, *Christ*: 5:1, 6). That assertion is at the heart of the Gospel and the lesson for this day (John 20:31; Acts 3:18). Jesus is also the Son of God (v. 5). Again, the Gospel reading makes the same point (John 20:31). Christianity, however, has to do not only with right believing, but also with right living. Using a typical Jewish expression, 1 John speaks about Christian living in terms of a walk, in fact walking "just as he walked" (2:6). The key word for this New Testament writer in describing that walk is "love," which comes up five times in this short pericope.

In these few words are directives to help keep the young church—and the church of our time—on the right course. What should we believe about Jesus? Jesus is the Messiah, the Son of God. How should those who believe in Jesus live? Statements a bit earlier fill in the answer more completely, putting ethics in the right perspective: "God sent his only Son so that we might live. . . . [God] sent his Son to be the atoning sacrifice for our sins . . . since God loved us so much, we also ought to love one another" (4:9-11). Theology, Christology, and ethics all fit together, and 1 John helps those who call themselves Christians to get that fit just right. 1 John is aimed at helping those who call themselves Christians to talk the right talk and to walk the right walk. This text is designed to help us post-Easter people keep on course.

## WHY READ THE BIBLE?
## JOHN 20:19-31

Since the Gospel texts for six out of the next seven Sundays, including Pentecost, are all from the Fourth Gospel, we begin with a comment about that Gospel as a whole. The text assigned for this Sunday provides us with a key to understanding these six pericopes, and indeed for understanding John's Gospel.

As the author comes to the conclusion of the Gospel, he wants readers to know that more could be told about this Jesus (v. 30). In fact, the final words of the book declare that if everything Jesus did were written down, the world itself could not contain all the books (21:25)!

Then the author lets us in on the purpose of his book. It is aimed at convincing those who read it (or who hear it read) that Jesus is the Messiah and also the Son of God. But why should the author wish to make this point? The answer is clear in the chapter's last words: "and that through believing you may have life in his name." Life: that is one of the key themes in this Gospel. On another occasion Jesus says, "I came that they may have life, and have it abundantly" (10:10; see also 3:15-16, 36; 5:24, 39-40; 6:40, 47, 53-54).

Thus it is clear that John is not just writing a doctrinal piece on Christology. His goal is not only to answer the question, Who is Jesus?—important as that question is. His is a more practical aim. He wants to show all who hear these words how they can find life, abundant life, meaningful life, even eternal life.

Apart from the conclusion in vv. 30-31, this pericope falls naturally into two scenes, taking place on the evening of Easter Sunday and that of the Sunday after Easter (19-25; 26-29).

John's postresurrection story had begun early on Sunday morning (20:1) and continues on the evening of that same day (20:19). The close followers of Jesus are gathered with the doors locked, "for fear of the Jews" (v. 19). As we read through John's Gospel, we discover that "the Jews" are increasingly portrayed as enemies of the followers of Jesus (1:19; 2:18, 20; 5:10, 15-16; 6:41, 52; 7:1, 11, 13; 9:18, 22; 10:24, 31, 33; 11:8; 13:33; 18:14). The figure of Nicodemus, the devout Jew who came to Jesus by night (chap. 3) should be kept in mind to counterbalance these references to Jewish opponents of Jesus. These anti-Jewish statements reflect a period in the history of the young church and should be read in that context. The church had its beginning with Jews who *did* believe in Jesus as Messiah.

Jesus greets his friends with words that remain the standard Jewish greeting to this day: *Shalom aleichem,* "Peace be with you." The Gospel account has already made the point that there was something different about Jesus after the resurrection; Mary did not recognize him (20:14-15). The same point was made in the story about the encounter on the road to Emmaus (Luke 24:15-16). While there was *identity*, the risen Christ was not *identical* with the preresurrection Jesus. This account illustrates another aspect of the "differentness" of Jesus after the resurrection: He appears in a room with locked doors. But it is the same Jesus. Look at the wounds in his hands and his side! With his appearance in their midst, the mood of the disciples quickly changes from fear to joy.

Jesus brings shalom, peace. Such is the point of the threefold repetition of that phrase. First, that shalom turned fear into joy. Now, the giving of that shalom is accompanied by the giving of the Holy Spirit. Jesus "breathed on them"; the Greek words are the same as those used in Gen. 2:7 when the Lord breathed the breath of life into the clod of clay that was the first human. God had given life to the first humans and now Jesus is giving a new kind of life to those gathered here. This has been called John's Pentecost story. It reflects a second way (cf. Acts 2) in which the church remembered receiving the Holy Spirit.

Many moderns will be able to identify with Thomas. He is the one who missed the meeting; for what reason, we do not know. No doubt he had another important commitment that evening. Thomas is also the one who is skeptical of hearsay and who draws his conclusions on the basis of careful examination of the evidence.

The fact that the disciples are gathered in the same place just a week later (the first Sunday after Easter) suggests a developing pattern of worship on Sunday, rather than on the Sabbath, the most important day on the Jewish calendar. Once again, the point about the difference in the resurrected Jesus is made: the doors were shut. Once again, we hear the same *Shalom aleichem*. This time Thomas is on hand. This busy skeptic does not take long to decide about Jesus. When he encounters the risen Jesus, his immediate reaction is, "My Lord and my God!" With this statement, John's view of Jesus comes full circle. Who is Jesus? Jesus is the Word, who was God, and who became flesh (1:1-14). The second scene ends with a word of commendation for those who believe in this Jesus even though they have not had the opportunity to encounter him in the way Thomas did.

We have dealt with the conclusion of our text at the beginning of this discussion. We now return to the thematic statement: Why read the Bible? John gives us a clue. We do not read because we are going to find abundant life in that book, as Jesus pointed out earlier (5:39). The Bible is not an answer book, nor is it a treasure chest of quotations letting us in on the secrets of the good life. We read the Bible because the Bible contains a collection of reports from those who had met Jesus firsthand. These reports point us to that person—called Messiah, Son of God—and promise that through him, we will find the sort of life we would all like to live. The readings from John from now through Pentecost will tell more about that life.

# Third Sunday of Easter

| Lutheran | Roman Catholic | Episcopal | Common Lectionary |
|---|---|---|---|
| Acts 4:8-12 | Acts 3:13-15, 17-19 | Acts 4:5-12 | Acts 3:12-19 |
| 1 John 1:1—2:2 | 1 John 2:1-5a | 1 John 1:1—2:2 | 1 John 3:1-7 |
| Luke 24:36-49 | Luke 24:35-48 | Luke 24:36b-48 | Luke 24:35-48 |

Those who have experienced earthquakes know that after the quake come the aftershocks. The texts for this Sunday may be viewed as aftershocks. Just two weeks ago we celebrated an event that generated such aftershocks that ever since, people have marked their calendars according to the birth of the one who was raised on that day. The Gospel for this Sunday presents us with another scene in Jerusalem, where the risen Christ appears to the disciples. The series of texts in Acts continues, again picking up the story of how the good news about Jesus begins to spread like wildfire across the world. 1 John provides reflection on the meaning of the death and resurrection of Jesus, focusing on the issues of our sins and shortcomings and of forgiveness.

## THE AFTERSHOCKS
## ACTS 4:8-12

This is the second of the apostolic speeches recorded in the early chapters of Acts. The first one was occasioned when a crowd gathered at the Jerusalem temple, after Peter and John had healed a lame man (Acts 3; see the discussion for the Second Sunday of Easter).

Acts 4:1-7 sets the scene for this next speech. Peter and John had caused a good deal of excitement. As Acts portrays them, they were announcing to this Jewish audience that the long-awaited Messiah had come in the person of Jesus, who had been crucified and now had risen from the dead. Central to their preaching or kerygma were the following themes: (1) The time of fullfilment of Scriptures has begun (2:16, 29-31; 3:18, 24); (2) the messianic promises have been fulfilled in the life, death, and resurrection of Jesus (2:22-24, 32-33; 3:13-15); (3) therefore repent, believe this good news, be baptized, and receive forgiveness of sins (2:37-38; 3:19). While some five thousand people in Jerusalem gladly heard the apostles and believed their message (4:4), the religious establishment was not so happy with what was going on. The Sadducees in particular were annoyed, because they denied any sort of resurrection of the dead (Acts 23:6-8; Matt. 22:23-33; cf. Acts 5:17). So they arranged to have Peter and John spend the night locked up in prison.

The next morning the apostles themselves were on trial, before an assembly called together by the high priest. The healing of the lame man was still in the background. The disciples were asked, "By what power or by what name did you do this?"

Some have suggested that this biblical book should be entitled, "The Acts of the Holy Spirit." The Pentecost story in Acts 2 tells of the coming of the Spirit, in the fulfillment of prophecy (2:1-21). The apostles were announcing that people could receive the gift of the Holy Spirit (2:38). And now, as Peter is about to speak, he is empowered by that Spirit (4:8).

Even in this short speech, the typical themes of the earliest apostolic preaching are evident: (1) the promises are being fulfilled (4:11); (2) in the person of Jesus the Christ or Messiah, crucified by the people and raised by God (4:10); (3) in whom salvation may be found (4:12).

Peter quotes from Psalm 118. This is the last of a series of psalms called the "Egyptian Hallel" and used by Jewish people to this day in connection with the celebration of Passover. Psalms 113 and 114 are sung before the meal; 114 recalls the exodus and crossing of the Red Sea and the Jordan River. Psalms 115–118 are sung after the Passover meal. Since the use of these psalms is an ancient tradition, we might expect that Jesus and his disciples sang them at the Passover celebrated just before the crucifixion (Mark 14:12-31). Psalm 118:17-18 speaks of resurrection; vv. 22-24 are often quoted in the New Testament (Matt. 21:42; 1 Pet. 2:7). Luther wrote, "This is my own beloved psalm. Although the entire Psalter and all of Holy Scripture are dear to me as my only comfort and source of life, I fell in love with this psalm especially" (*Luther's Works*, 14:45).

It would have been likely that Peter sang this psalm with Jesus at that memorable Passover celebration just before the crucifixion. In it he found a picture of just what had happened to Jesus: the one who was rejected has now received the place of honor and importance (Matt. 21:42; Mark 12:10; 1 Pet. 2:7)

## DOWN-TO-EARTH RELIGION
## 1 JOHN 1:1—2:2

The series of lessons from 1 John continues with this second selection from that book; for introductory comments, see the remarks on 1 John 5:1-6 for the Second Sunday of Easter. We have said that the purpose of this treatise, written after the time of the apostles and in the early years of the history of the church, was to keep the young church on course. This letter hints at two burning questions in this church: First, who is Jesus? Some were claiming that Jesus was not truly human, but only seemed to be so; these were called the Docetists, from the Greek *dokeo*, "seem." Second, how should we live? There were some who apparently did not think that obeying the commandments was of major importance for the Christian life (1 John 1:6; 2:4-6).

Who is this Jesus? This was an issue for Jesus' contemporaries (Mark 8:27) and continues to be a question for those debating the issue and writing volumes on Christology to this day. Early in the church's history, there were those who denied that Jesus was truly human. The opening words of 1 John appear to be directed toward them. "From the beginning" echoes the opening of the Fourth Gospel. But while John 1 emphasizes the otherness of the Word that was "with God" even "in the beginning," the opening of this letter stresses the fact that the "word of life" was among human beings for a time. Jesus was no remote heavenly spirit, but a down-to-earth, real person. The writer of 1 John says of him, "we have heard, we have seen, we have looked at and touched with our hands." The context that called forth 1 John made it important to describe Jesus as a human being who lived among other human beings who could tell what Jesus was like.

Another important theme is introduced in the opening of this letter. The author speaks of *koinōnia*, related to the verb meaning "to share, have a share in," and translated as "fellowship." The author desires that those whom he addresses will have *koinōnia* with himself and others in his group. This fellowship, he says, is really a relationship both to the Father and the Son Jesus Christ (1:3).

The *koinonia* theme continues into 1:5-10. Those who are Christian have fellowship with God (v. 6) and also with one another (v. 7). Those in this community have experienced God's love and then pass that love on to others. Later on, the writer will say that Christians are people who have been loved by God and then in turn love one another (4:7-21).

The theme "God is light" (1:5) recalls the opening of John's Gospel (1:4-9). One of the popular songs during World War II expressed longing for those days when the darkness of war would be dispelled, "When the lights go on again, all over the world." The Fourth Gospel pictures Jesus in this way, as the light coming into the world, enlightening everyone (1:8-9). That same imagery occurs here.

The triple "if we say" appears to be aimed at those in the community who are not keeping on the right theological course. They apparently claim fellowship with God but their lives do not show it, and so they turn out to be liars (1:6). They claim, it seems, to have reached a certain degree of moral perfection (vv. 8, 10).

This letter is not aimed at those who consider themselves to have attained perfection. It is addressed to those who know themselves to be failures. The Greek word for sin here is *hamartia*, which has the sense of "missing the target." The Old Testament (LXX) uses the word in describing the seven hundred left-handed slingshotters from the tribe of Benjamin, who could fire a stone at a hair and not miss the target (Judg. 20:16). Note that John assumes that he is addressing a group of Christians who know what it is to miss the target, to fail to live up to the expectations of their own biblical tradition. The bad news, says the writer, is that we are all failures (1:8). To claim to be otherwise is to make God a liar and is an indication that God's word is really not living in us (1:10). The good news, however, is that even though we have all fallen short of our own expectations or of someone else's or of God's, there is a way out. When we are called before God's own court, we have an advocate. That representative is Jesus Christ, whose blood cleans us up and whose death was the sacrifice for our sins. Like the writer of the Fourth Gospel, this writer thinks big: What Jesus did has implications for the whole world (1 John 2:1-2; John 3:16).

This text has some important things to say about sin and forgiveness, amplifying what Jesus says on the same theme in the Gospel for this Sunday (Luke 24:47).

In sum: This letter, coming from a time after the Gospels and Paul's letters had been written, demonstrates the importance of keeping the ship of the church on course. This particular text reminds us that Christianity is a practical, down-to-earth faith. Jesus came down to earth in human form. The Christian life is described as walking—again, a down-to-earth picture (1:7; cf. 2:6). The Christian community ought to be marked by mutual concern for one another, later to be expressed simply as love for one another (1 John 4:7-21). A part of the life of the community is the acknowledgment of failure, of sin, and the reception of cleansing and forgiveness (1:8—2:2).

## DYNAMITE!
## LUKE 24:36-49

The text for this Sunday presents us with a third postresurrection scene where Jesus appears. All three scenes take place on the same Easter Sunday: (1) at the empty tomb (24:1-12); (2) on the road to Emmaus (24:13-35); (3) in a room in Jerusalem (vv. 36-49). The last two have the following common elements: (1) Jesus appears (15, 36); (2) Jesus is not immediately recognized (16, 37); (3) the disciples are criticized for their doubts (25, 38); (4) Jesus leads a Bible study (27, 45); (5) food is eaten (30, 42-43).

The first two appearances have been discussed in connection with the texts for Easter Evening. The focus for this Sunday is on the incident in the room in Jerusalem, in the evening of a most remarkable day. The lectionary invites us to look back, one more time, at the events of that first Easter Sunday, including things that Jesus did (36-43, where action is central) and things that Jesus said (44-49, all words of Jesus).

36-43. The scene here is reminiscent of that described in John 20. In two instances, the NRSV includes words that were placed in footnotes in the RSV (vv. 36, 40); in any case, the words have parallels in John 20:19-20 and no doubt reflect authentic early tradition. John said that the doors were locked (20:19); here it is simply reported that Jesus stood among them. In both cases, the emphasis is on the fact that there is an element of difference, of discontinuity, between the resurrected Christ and Jesus. The Greek behind "ghost" is *pneuma,* translated as "spirit" in the RSV. In the appearance story of John 20, Mary recognized Jesus when she spoke his name; in the Emmaus story, the pair of travelers recognized Jesus in the breaking of bread. Now Jesus invites the disciples to touch him, showing them his hands and feet with the nail marks on them. Thus there is also sameness, continuity, between the risen Christ and Jesus. Each of these postresurrection texts makes the point that while there is identity between Jesus and the risen Christ, Christ's resurrected body is not identical with the preresurrection body.

"A ghost does not have flesh and bones," says Jesus. This incident adds another detail to the picture of the resurrected Christ: he eats food in a normal manner. This is no hallucination or disembodied spirit. This is Jesus the Messiah, executed and now raised from the dead.

There is something of a progression as we watch the reactions of those who encounter the evidence of the risen Christ in Luke's portrayal of Easter day. When they first encountered the empty tomb, the followers of Jesus were perplexed and then terrified, not understanding what had happened to Jesus, and in fact not believing that the tomb was empty (24:4-5, 11-12). When the Emmaus travelers arrived in Jerusalem, their friends were talking about Jesus' resurrection (24:34-35). Now, when Jesus actually appears among them, their emotions are a mixture of wonder, disbelief, and joy (41).

The second part of the text for this Sunday consists of words of Jesus. They summarize events of the past but also point toward the future. "These are my words" looks back at "all that Jesus did and taught from the beginning," as presented in Luke's Gospel (Acts 1:1). The Hebrew Bible or Old Testament is traditionally divided into Torah, Prophets, and Writings, the last section beginning with the Psalms. The comment in 24:44 assumes these three divisions, as does 24:27.

The Old Testament presents a picture of a coming messianic ruler who will be victorious in battle, rule all nations, rule forever, and in fact be seated at the right hand of God (Psalms 2, 72, 110). These texts, along with promises such as those in Isaiah 7, 9, and 11 and Micah 5, all contributed to the expectation of a triumphant, politically powerful Messiah. However, the Old Testament also portrays a future figure who will accomplish God's mission through suffering (Isa. 42:1-4; 49:1-6; 50:4-11; 52:13—53:12).

Everyone reading these pages would love to have heard what Jesus said in the Bible studies he conducted on that first Easter Sunday, one on the road, another in this room in Jerusalem. What texts did he read? What did he say about them? One would certainly suspect that in addition to the usual messianic texts listed above, Jesus read those servant poems from the book of Isaiah 42–53, pointing out that the expected Messiah was not only a triumphant figure, but that "his Messiah would suffer" (Acts 3:18). Thus Jesus was indeed Messiah—but a different sort of Messiah than many had expected. He was a Messiah who suffered and died and then was raised from the dead.

We have noted above the three fundamental themes running through the early sermons in Acts (see the comments on Acts 4:8-12). These same themes are evident in this wind-up of Luke's Gospel: the prophecies are being fulfilled (24:44) in the life, death, and resurrection of Jesus Messiah (45-46), calling for repentance and making possible forgiveness and a fresh start (47). This is, in a nutshell, what the good news is all about.

Then Jesus gives a hint about the future. This good news is not to be kept in Jerusalem, but is to be taken "to all nations." How could these ordinary people be involved in such a charge? The word that ends v. 49 in the Greek original expresses it. Wait a while, Jesus says. Stay here in Jersualem for a bit. "Until you are clothed from on high with power," reads the Greek literally. The word for power here is *dynamis*, from which we get the words "dynamic" and "dynamite."

So wait a while, says Jesus. It won't be long until you'll be latched up with a power like dynamite, a power that will cause an evangelism explosion taking the good news from Jersualem to the ends of the earth. We're hearing about that evangelism explosion in the texts from Acts for these Sundays.

# Fourth Sunday of Easter

| Lutheran | Roman Catholic | Episcopal | Common Lectionary |
|----------|----------------|-----------|-------------------|
| Acts 4:23-33 | Acts 4:8-12 | Acts 4:32-37 | Acts 4:8-12 |
| 1 John 3:1-2 | 1 John 3:1-2 | 1 John 3:1-8 | 1 John 3:18-24 |
| John 10:11-18 | John 10:11-18 | John 10:11-16 | John 10:11-18 |

The texts for this Sunday are rich in imagery. The Gospel pictures Jesus as the good shepherd (and portrays believers as sheep). The reading from 1 John pictures Christians as a family, as children of a heavenly father. The scene in Acts from the life of the young church calls us to tell the story of our faith with boldness and with imagination.

## PRAYER CHANGES THINGS
## ACTS 4:23-33

Our tour through the Book of Acts continues. Like the texts for the previous two Sundays (3:13-15, 17-26; 4:8-12), this one has its setting in Jerusalem, reporting further reactions to the healing of the lame man in the temple. The leaders of the Jerusalem community are described as "annoyed" (4:2) by what was going on in their city. They had arrested John and Peter after the commotion following the healing of the lame man and had put them in jail. When called to explain their actions, Peter gave an inspired accounting, coming to a climax in the declaration that salvation was to be found only in Jesus (4:8-12). The city leaders were perplexed. Standing alongside these troublemakers was a man in his forties who had been lame and now was cured. No one could deny that marvelous healing had taken place. But Peter and John were causing too much disturbance of the peace, so the leaders ordered them to stop teaching or speaking in the name of Jesus. "We have to tell about what we have seen and heard," was their reply. The crowd was on the side of Peter and John and the man who was healed, so there was nothing to do but let them go.

At this point the text for this Sunday picks up the story. It begins with a narrative framework, telling how Peter and John return to the other disciples with the report that they had been told not to teach or speak about Jesus (4:23-24a). The main part of the pericope is a prayer, prayed together by these earliest disciples (4:24b-30). The narrative records the results of that prayer (v. 31). The pericope closes with the first part of one of the summaries in Acts (4:32-35; see also 1:14; 2:42-47; 5:12-16; 6:7; 9:31-32) tying together the story told thus far (4:32-33).

Our congregational prayers begin, "Let us pray for the whole people of God in Christ Jesus, and for all people according to their needs." How should we pray together in worship? This text presents us with one of the earliest examples of congregational prayer in the young church. What can we learn about prayer from it? The prayer consists of an address (v. 24b), a recalling of what God had said in Psalm 2 and of what God had been doing in Jerusalem (vv. 25-28), and a specific request (vv. 29-30).

God is addressed as "sovereign Lord" (in Greek, *Despota*). The sense of the word is "master," picturing those praying as servants and God as their master (see 2 Tim. 2:21, "owner"; also Titus 2:9, "masters"). The same address appears in Simeon's prayer in the temple, making explicit the servant/master relationship (Luke 2:29). These early Christians view God as their master— and can also speak of Jesus Christ in the same language (Jude 4). The words, "who made the heaven and the earth, the sea, and everything in them," are Old Testament language, recalling passages such as Exod. 20:11 and Ps. 146:6.

How ought we to pray as a congregation? This text suggests that we begin by keeping straight who we are and who God is: God is the master, we are the servants. Those who pray get their bearings for their present situation by looking back at what God has done in their past. First, they recall God's power over nature, calling to mind what God has done as creator. As the prayer continues, they continue their focus on the past by recalling what God had said, in this case citing Psalm 2. That royal psalm, used in the time of the monarchy in connection with the coronation of a new king, spoke about kings and rulers gathering against the Lord and his "anointed" or, in Hebrew, Messiah. This group of early believers in Jesus as Messiah sees precisely such a conflict going on in their own time. The kings and rulers of their day gathered against Jesus, "whom you anointed." The Greek is *echrisas*, related to the word *christos*, which means anointed one, or Christ. And all of these events, these believers confess, happened according to God's plan (4:28).

The prayer comes to the point with the "and now" that introduces v. 29. The same expression introduces the request in the prayer of 2 Chron. 20:10 ("See now," NRSV) and also Isa. 37:20 ("So now," NRSV). These "servants" (continuing the master/servant imagery) ask for "boldness." Remember, they have been ordered not to speak (4:16-18). We have already noted the "boldness" that marked Peter's speech (4:13). The apostles pray that they might speak courageously, and that God will act powerfully, with healings (such as had just taken place in the healing of the lame man) and further "signs and wonders" (2:43; 5:12; 6:8; 7:36; 14:3; 15:12).

This congregational prayer had dramatic results (4:31). The house shook, like a house shakes in a terrible storm (cf. Luke 6:48). The disciples had asked that they might speak God's word with boldness; they are now empowered by the Holy Spirit to do just that. Once again the coming of the Holy Spirit is associated with the receiving of power (Acts 1:8; cf. 4:32).

Verses 32-33 summarize the story to this point. These earliest Christians shared everything they had with one another. And now they continued to speak with power, telling the story of the resurrection.

"Prayer Changes Things." Many a farmhouse in the Midwest where I grew up had a carefully embroidered cloth on the wall with these words. Here is a clear example of the nature of congregational prayer in the earliest church. What could we learn from this example, in regard to our own praying together? (1) When God's people are in a tough situation, they pray. These early Christians are experiencing all sorts of opposition, precisely from those who believe in the same God (4:29; cf. 2 Chron. 20:1-3 and Isa. 37:1-4). (2) The relationship between the ones speaking and the one addressed is clear. God is portrayed as master, with the power to control nature (v. 24) and history (v. 28) and those praying as servants. (3) The prayer is rooted in the biblical tradition of prayer, addressing God in biblical language and growing out of one of the Psalms. (4) This particular prayer did not result in God removing the difficulties, but did result in God giving the apostles boldness and power to continue their work.

# WHO DO WE THINK WE ARE?
## 1 JOHN 3:1-2

We have already noted in connection with the text for the Second Sunday of Easter that the purpose of 1 John is to help keep the young church on course. The half-dozen texts from 1 John that come up during this Easter season are all concerned with providing direction to the first Christians on matters of what to believe and how to live. Who was this Jesus? How ought his followers to live? The short selection assigned for this Sunday provides some guidance on another basic question: How should we as believers in Jesus as the Messiah understand ourselves? Or, to put the question another way, who do we think we are?

Anyone reading this letter is immediately struck by the way in which the author addresses the audience: "My little children," he says in 2:1; that same "little children" (Greek, *teknia,* diminutive of *teknon*) comes up seven times throughout the letter, in 2:12, 28; 3:7, 18; 4:4; and 5:21. Just after Judas had left, Jesus addressed the eleven disciples in the same way, "Little children, I am with you only a little longer" (John 13:33). The expression is used in some manuscripts at Gal. 4:19 (others read simply "children"); these are the only occurrences in the New Testament. The Gospel of John and especially 1 John thus show a preference for using this sort of family language in reference to fellow believers.

Someone once said that the New Testament writings do not present us with a carefully formulated doctrine of the church, but rather show us a gallery of pictures. Ephesians, for example, shows us the church as Christ's body (1:23), as God's family (2:19), as a building (2:20-21), as a temple (2:21-22), as

God's bride (5:23). In the Sermon on the Mount, Jesus spoke of his followers as salt and light (Matt. 5:13-14), as a mustard seed, and as leaven (Matt. 13:31-33). The list can be extended. Each picture brings out a different aspect of the church. Each provides an answer to the question of those who are members of the church: Who do we think we are?

The author of 1 John calls God "Father" (1:2, 3; 2:1, 14, 15, 22; 3:1; 4:14). He suggests that the believers in Jesus as Messiah to whom he is writing call themselves "children of God" (3:1, 2). Here is yet another picture that helped the young church to understand itself. Who do we think we are? We are children of God. God is our Father.

Surprisingly, the picture of God as Father or as Parent does not come up often in the Old Testament. It usually refers to the relationship between God and the people Israel (Deut. 32:6; Isa. 1:2; 63:16; 64:8; Mal. 1:6; 2:10); in Ps. 103:13 it occurs in a more individual way. With Jesus, however, things change. "Father" becomes a typical designation for God (e.g., Matt. 5:45, 48; 6:4, 6, 9, 14, 15).

If Christians refer to God as Father, this has two implications: believers are children who relate to God as a parent, and believers relate to other Christians as brothers and sisters. Who do we think we are, as first-century believers, or as believers in the twentieth century? The answer in this text is clear: We are children of God.

I recall preaching on the notion of the church as family of God, and saying that this means that we could quite rightly refer to one another as "brother George" or "sister Martha." After the service, as I was shaking hands at the door, a small girl, maybe ten years old, gave my hand a good shake, looked me in the eye, and said, "Good morning, brother!" She had been listening.

My teacher Gerhard Frost once told about teaching the Lord's Prayer to a group of young children. He asked them, "What should we do with our hands when we pray?" The children quickly folded their hands, with the exception of one. She wanted the whole group to hold hands—because, she said, the prayer does not say, "my Father," but "Our Father." She understood.

This text gives us an important picture of the church: the church is a family. This tells us something about our relationship to God: God is our Father, or Parent, who loves us and has our best interests at heart. It also tells us something about our relationship to one another: sitting next to me in church is brother Pete, or sister Sue. Individuals in families are not all alike. Some may like Beethoven, while others prefer Garth Brooks or Spinal Tap. We all know the dangers of trying to act as if all children in a family are alike. But families are linked together by a love for parents and a love for one another. So it ought to be in our own families. So it ought to be in the family of God, the church, who have brothers and sisters who care and who need care (Acts 4:32), and who have a heavenly Father who loves them. This scene out of the life of the young church reminds us of the power of common prayer and calls us to telling the story about the Lord Jesus with imagination and boldness.

## WHO DO WE THINK WE ARE? (CONTINUED)
## JOHN 10:11-18

The Gospel for this Sunday provides us with one of the powerful pictures of Jesus, and of ourselves. Jesus is the Good Shepherd and we as believers are sheep.

A stroll through the stacks of a seminary library introduces one to an amazing collection of books dealing with the question, "Who is Jesus?" They are listed under the topic "Christology." Seminary catalogs list courses on the same theme. One way in which the Bible deals with that question is to provide a number of pictures to understand who Jesus is. Some of the most important are found in the "I am" statements of the Fourth Gospel. Jesus says: I am the bread of life (6:35), the light of the world (8:12; 9:5), the gate for the sheep (10:7), the good shepherd (10:11, 14), the resurrection and the life (11:25), the way, the truth, and the life (14:6), and the true vine (15:1).

Jesus did not invent the Good Shepherd picture. The imagery has its roots in the Old Testament. The prophet of the exile addressed those in Babylon, preaching comfort to them (Isa 40:1) and picturing a new exodus, when they would stream out of captivity and return home. One of the images used to convey this message was that of the Lord as shepherd, the people as sheep (Isa. 40:11). Jeremiah used the same imagery, contrasting the Lord's future shepherding care with the irresponsible actions of Israel's present kings or "shepherds" (Jer. 23:1-4). Ezekiel chastised Israel's present kings, speaking of a future when the Lord would come as the good shepherd (Ezekiel 34; note esp. vv. 11-16).

The most famous portrayal of God as shepherd is Psalm 23, the psalm assigned for this Sunday. This is often called a "psalm of trust" and should be understood against the background of the lament psalms, taking the element of trust from that psalm type and developing it into an entire psalm. Note the expression "for you are with me" in v. 4. At this point, the psalmist shifts from talking *about* God (vv. 1-3) to speaking *to* God as "you." In the Hebrew original, there are twenty-six words that lead up to this expression; following it are another twenty-six words. This centering device highlights the central point of the psalm.

Other Gospels report Jesus speaking of himself as shepherd (Matt. 18:12-14; Luke 15:3-7), but here the imagery is developed the most fully. After calling himself the bread of life (6:35, 48) and the light of the world (8:12; 9:5), Jesus now uses imagery from the work of tending sheep. He pictures himself as the gate through which believers enter into life with God and then return again to following him in the world (10:1-6). We may note the following themes in the section portraying Jesus as good shepherd:

First, Jesus says that he is the good shepherd, which means that he will give his life for his sheep entrusted to his care. Psalm 23 portrayed the shepherd as sticking with the sheep through the trials of the darkest valley. In Jesus' portrayal, the good shepherd not only stays with his sheep in difficult times but lays down his life for them. Here Jesus is pointing to his work on the cross. The first segment of this shepherd speech is bracketed by the reference to the shepherd laying down his life for his sheep (vv. 11, 15).

Second, v. 16 strikes a wide-hearted note. The Fourth Gospel was written long after the events it described took place. By the time it was published, Paul had written his letters and young churches were flourishing in places like Jerusalem, Antioch, and Corinth. Jesus as portrayed here acknowledges that the barn where he keeps his sheep is not a narrow, isolated, insulated one. The "other sheep" is most likely a reference to Christians who did not come out of a Jewish background. They, too, are part of this flock. Here is one of the Bible's clear expressions of hope for one worldwide—that is, ecumenical—church (see also Eph. 2:11-22; 4:1-6).

Third, Jesus says that as the good shepherd, he volunteered to give his life for the sheep, carrying out a directive from his Father (10:18).

If Jesus is shepherd, that means that we as followers of Jesus ought to see ourselves as sheep. This is the other half of the picture, which we can quite easily forget. Sheep are not necessarily noted for their intelligence or bravery. Nor are they known as good leaders. They are in fact followers (10:3-5). I personally have attended many a leadership retreat; the text here suggests that we really ought to have a session or two focusing on followership. Jesus' characteristic call, we know, was not "listen to me" or even "believe me," but rather, like the call of a shepherd to sheep, "follow me."

# Fifth Sunday of Easter

| Lutheran | Roman Catholic | Episcopal | Common Lectionary |
|----------|----------------|-----------|-------------------|
| Acts 8:26-40 | Acts 9:26-31 | Acts 8:26-40 | Acts 8:26-40 |
| 1 John 3:18-24 | 1 John 3:18-24 | 1 John 3:18-24 | 1 John 4:7-12 |
| John 15:1-8 | John 15:1-8 | John 14:15-21 | John 15:1-8 |

The preacher has the choice of three fine texts for this Sunday. The account in Acts tells one of the unforgettable mission stories from the early church. The lesson continues the series of instructional texts from 1 John, while the Gospel centers on one of the great metaphors for Jesus.

## ON THE ROAD AGAIN
## ACTS 8:26-40

The theme for the story told in Acts was struck in 1:8, when Jesus promised the apostles that they would receive power from the Holy Spirit and be witnesses "in Jerusalem, in all Judea and Samaria, and to the ends of the earth." The snapshots from Acts for the past three Sundays have all focused on scenes that took place in Jerusalem, just after the healing of a lame man in the temple area. Acts 8 reports on Philip's words and actions in Samaria, where he preached to crowds and also did miracles. The result of his work was that "there was great joy in that city" (8:5-8). The pericope for this Sunday tells another story about Philip, this time zeroing in on an encounter with one individual. Again, Philip's work consists of proclamation and an act (word and sacrament), and the account ends on a note of joy (8:39). The story continues to move outward from Jerusalem, now taking place on the road to Gaza to the southwest and ending in Azotus (Ashdod) and Caesarea to the north.

The story is told in a manner reminiscent of accounts about the Old Testament prophets. Just as Elijah was told to "get up and go" and he "got up and went" (1 Kings 17:8-10, literal translation), so Philip was directed and so he did (vv. 26-27). The Lord is guiding the action here, through an angel (v. 26) or the Spirit (vv. 29, 39). In Acts, the Lord's messenger or angel may perform wondrous deeds as well as speak (5:19-20; 12:6-11; 27:23-24; cf. 7:30).

This story involves two characters. Philip is on foot, heading down the road leading to Gaza to the southwest of Jerusalem. The other character in the story is not named. We do know that he was from the far-off kingdom of Ethiopia, and therefore black. The commentators debate whether being called a eunuch necessarily meant he had been castrated; in any case, he was a high official in the court of the queen, known as "the Candace." Had the eunuch converted to Judaism? This seems likely, but the text is not clear. The story does tell us that he had been on a religious pilgrimage to Jerusalem. Now, on his way home, seated in his government vehicle, he was reading from the Isaiah scroll.

The first directive given to Philip was to head down the road to Gaza. The Spirit directs him to run over toward the chariot coming down the road. Why should he do that? When he got near, the reason was clear. He heard the passenger reading aloud. He listened for a moment and recognized what was being read as a portion of the prophet Isaiah. The timing was perfect. Philip had already spent considerable time proclaiming Jesus to be the Messiah (8:5). When he heard the distinguished traveler reading words from Isaiah 53, he could not help but comment. "Do you understand what that text really means?" he asked. "No" was the answer, "I need some help." So the rider invites Philip to hop up in his chariot, and the two of them proceed down the road, engaged in the first Bible study on wheels recorded in Christian history.

After reading the text, the eunuch asked the question that so many have asked in connection with Isaiah 53: "Who is the servant spoken about here? The prophet? Or somebody else?"

Philip recognized the teachable moment. This text gave him the opportunity to tell about Jesus. We have only the briefest hint of what he said. Whatever it was, it included something about being baptized (see Acts 2:38). Philip's explanation must have been compelling. This high-ranking government official, who had taken the time to make a religious pilgrimage, recognized an important opportunity when it came. When the chariot neared a stream, he ordered the driver to stop. They got out, went down into the water, the official was baptized, and the Christian faith was on its way into Ethiopia.

The story concludes quickly. The third mention of the angel/Spirit of the Lord tells how Philip is whisked away to carry on his work at Azotus (the old Philistine city of Ashdod) and in Caesarea. In the meantime, the eunuch continues the long ride to his homeland, now going on his way rejoicing. We hear nothing further about him. Once again, Philip had brought reason for joy to those with whom he worked (8:8).

This account stands as a reminder that the great moments in the story of God and humankind do not all take place in temples or synagogues or churches. Somehow the good news about Jesus had a way of breaking out of the confines of the usual religious structures. Luke had already told one postresurrection "road story" about an unforgettable Bible study that took place on the road to the town of Emmaus (Luke 24:13-35). Here the story about Jesus is again told in an unusual setting, to an unusual audience. Philip, who had a somewhat unusual family that included four unmarried prophesying daughters (Acts 21:8-9), carried out his assignment while riding in a government vehicle heading for Africa. Teacher and student were on the road again. The previous Lukan road story concluded with a reminiscence of the celebration of the Lord's Supper; this one concludes with a baptism.

Centuries earlier, a psalmist had pictured life with God as a journey (Psalm 121, esp. vv. 7-8). The writer to the Hebrews saw the Christian life this way (Hebrews 11, esp. vv. 9-10, 13-14). And Jesus? When he gathered disciples, his call was not "listen to me" or even "believe in me," but rather "follow me." Life as a journey: this is one picture of Christian existence. Perhaps it is not without significance that the early Christians were called those who belonged to "the Way" (Acts 9:2; 19:9, 23; 24:22).

## WHAT'S IT ALL ABOUT?
## 1 JOHN 3:18-24

This is the fourth in the series of a half-dozen texts from 1 John in this post-Easter period. Some introductory comments have been provided in connection with the text for the Second Sunday of Easter. The lessons for this Sunday and the next (1 John 4:1-11) take a section out of the heart of John's letter. This letter helped to keep the young church on course, spelling out what these "children of God" (3:1-2) ought to believe, especially about Jesus, and also indicating something of how they ought to live. On these fifth and sixth Sundays of Easter, as we are once more trying to assimilate the significance of those events on that Easter Sunday, this letter can remind us again how these twin themes fit together: faith and ethics, right believing and right living.

Our segment for this Sunday begins with the fourth of seven times that the author addresses the audience as "little children" (*teknia*; 2:1, 12, 28; 3:7, 18; 4:4; 5:21). Twice this "little children" label introduces words about sin and forgiveness through Jesus Christ (2:1, 12). Four times "little children" appears before imperatives, instructing these young Christians in how to live (2:28, "abide in him"; 3:7, "let no one deceive you"; 3:18, "let us love"; 5:21, "keep yourselves from idols"). Once "little children" is used in connection with a reminder of who these people are (4:4).

The author uses family language throughout 1 John: "beloved" (*agapētoi*, 2:7; 3:2, 21; 4:1, 7, 11); "children" (*paidia*, 2:18; variant in some manuscripts for *teknia* in 3:7); "children of God" (*tekna theou*), 3:1, 2, 10; 5:2). All of this gives a particularly intimate flavor to this letter. The same "children" language appears in 2 John 1, 4, and 13 and in 3 John 2, 11 ("beloved"), and 4 ("children"). Such family language conveys not only a close relationship to God the Father, but also stands as a reminder that others in the Christian community are viewed as brothers and sisters (see the comments on 3:1-2 for the Fourth Sunday of Easter).

The statement in 3:23 stands at the center of this pericope and indeed at the center of 1 John:

> And this is his commandment,
>> that we should believe in the name
>>> of his Son Jesus Christ
>> and love one another,
> just as he has commanded us.

References to God's commandment frame the central statement here. What is the Christian life all about? What is its shape? Here it is all boiled down to two dimensions: belief in God's Son, Jesus Christ, and love toward one another. 1 John 4:21 speaks of love of God and love of brothers and sisters; 4:11 indicates the motivation for belief in Jesus and love toward one another: "since God loved us so much, we also ought to love one another."

Now what would this love for one another look like? We have seen that some in the group splintering off from the Christian community seemed to think that right living was not of great consequence (2:4). They are judged as living in the darkness (1:6; 2:9, 11; see the comments for the Second Sunday of Easter). But the "little children" statement in 3:18 makes clear that loving one another means more than just talk: "let us love, not in word or speech, but in truth and action." This will not be mere pious blather about love. As Eliza Doolittle sings in *My Fair Lady*, "Don't talk of stars burning above/if you're in love/show me!" At this point the author, who speaks so much of love, sounds very much like James, who says of pious words to a hungry and cold brother or sister, "What is the good of that?" (James 2:14-17). Love which shows itself in action is in fact a sign that we are rightly related to God (1 John 3:19).

With the address "Beloved," v. 21 introduces a new thought. We can come before God with a certain "boldness"; the same idea is expressed in 5:14. This is the attitude that Peter and John showed when they spoke before the crowds in Jerusalem (Acts 2:29; 4:13, 31). It is also an attitude that Christians can have, because of what Jesus Christ has done (Eph. 3:11-12; Heb. 4:14-16; 10:19 "confidence"). 1 John says that believers who abide in the Son and the Father may face Christ's second coming with this same boldness/confidence (2:28; see also 4:17).

After this reference to love for one another, the section ends with some thoughts about the relationship to Jesus Christ, now expressed in terms of "abiding" in him (v. 24). Precisely this notion is portrayed in the imagery of the vine and branches in this Sunday's Gospel text.

What's it all about? Such is the question we have asked in the title to this section. Christianity is first of all about belief in Jesus Christ, sent into the world to take care of our sins (3:23, expanded in 4:9-10). It is also about love for one another, a love that goes beyond talk, beyond words, to action. We shall discover more of these same themes in the next section of 1 John, to be considered next week.

# THIS CHRISTIAN LIFE, PART ONE
## JOHN 15:1-8

The lectionary that guides our preaching during this season between Easter and Pentecost now narrows its focus. The fifteenth chapter of John—more exactly, a part of this chapter—is worth concentrating on for two Sundays.

What is so important about John 15? Once again, we have a lesson in Christology combined with one in ecclesiology. Last week it was Jesus as shepherd and Christians as sheep. For the next two weeks the picture is of Jesus as vine and believers as branches.

The texts for three Sundays in a row are taken from the same section of John's Gospel. These are the words of Jesus delivered to his disciples as they are gathered at Passover time in Jerusalem, just before the crucifixion. We should keep in mind the drama of this situation. Imagine a coach making a final speech to eleven players just before the start of the Super Bowl. Here is Jesus with the eleven (Judas leaves; 13:30), saying what needs to be said just before the events that would change the history of life on this planet. John reports an act of Jesus (the footwashing, chap. 13) but his major concern is with Jesus' last words to his gathered followers (chaps. 14–16) and Jesus' prayer for them (chap. 17). We recognize the address, "little children" (13:33), found in the Gospels only here but often in 1 John. We hear words of comfort addressed to those who were (understandably) confused about what the future will bring (chap. 14). We listen in on Jesus as he prays for this band of believers, but also for the church of the future (chap. 17, esp. vv. 20-21). And Jesus provides yet another picture to help these disciples (and "those who will believe in me through their word," 17:20) to understand their life as Christians in the world.

That life is described in terms of three basic relationships: the believers and Christ (15:1-11), the believers and one another (15:12-17), and the believers and the world (15:18—16:33). Our task for this Sunday is to listen to this instruction about believers and their relationship to Christ. According to 17:20-21, these materials were written for people who have something in common with us: They have come to believe through the words of others. Now some instruction on the fundamentals for those eleven.

We have noted the series of "I am" statements in John in connection with the discussion of John 10 (Fourth Sunday of Easter). This is now the last of these statements. "I am the true vine," says Jesus, "and my Father is the vinegrower." Commentators fill pages with learned speculation about the background of this imagery. Those living in first-century Palestine must have seen sheep every day (John 10) and if they walked out in the country, they saw vineyards. The imagery was a natural one for preachers and prophets with a pedagogical eye, ever on the prowl for illustrative material to make a point. The prophets spoke of vineyards (Isa. 5:1-7; 27:2-5; Jer. 2:21; Ezek. 15:1-8; 19:10-14), as did historians (Judg. 9:8-15) and psalmists (Ps. 80:8-13). Had Jesus lived in midwestern America during the twentieth century, he would probably have spoken about corn or soybeans.

The pericope falls into two sections, each introduced by "I am the vine": vv. 1-4 and 5-8. Perhaps the imagery came to mind because Jesus and the disciples were drinking wine together. An aside: As I walked down a forest road thinking about this text, I saw a huge branch from a birch tree that had broken off the main trunk in a windstorm a couple of weeks earlier. It hung there, its leaves brown, withering away. The picture in the first section of this text is as simple as that. Christians then (one thinks of Judas, 13:26-30) and now can produce nothing on their own, without being connected to their source of nourishment and power. They are like the branch of that birch tree, cut off, decaying, dead. The point? "Abide in me," says Jesus, "as I abide in you." The lesson from 1 John for today told us something about what that "abiding" means.

As all speakers and preachers know, skillful use of repetition is the way to emphasize a point. So here it is again, in v. 5: "I am the vine, you are the branches." Verse 6 shows us that dead birch branch once again, hanging there lifeless, withering away. Soon it will have to be cleared away and burned. Verse 5 pictures the life of one connected to the source of nourishment, of power. That life is far from shriveled up, decaying, or dying, but is marked by bearing fruit; we hear more about that in next week's text (15:16). Paul uses the same imagery in Gal. 5:22-23. The life of the one who "abides in me" (again in v. 7) is also marked by access to God the Father. Pray—and God will hear your prayers, says Jesus (v. 7).

Jesus began by declaring himself to be the vine and identifying his Father as the farmer or vinedresser. Now, at the end of this pericope, he speaks of his Father once again. A well-tended field, free of weeds, heavy with the harvest, is a certain credit to the farmer who has planted and cared for it. In the same way, says Jesus, the lives of faithful and fruit-bearing disciples offer up praise to their heavenly Father.

# Sixth Sunday of Easter

| Lutheran | Roman Catholic | Episcopal | Common Lectionary |
|---|---|---|---|
| Acts 11:19-30 | Acts 10:25-26, 34-35, 44-48 | Acts 11:19-30 | Acts 10:44-48 |
| 1 John 4:1-11 | 1 John 4:7-10 | 1 John 4:7-21 | 1 John 5:1-6 |
| John 15:9-17 | John 15:9-17 | John 15:9-17 | John 15:9-17 |

The good news continues to get out, like a flame spreading across the Mediterranean world. The first lesson continues the series of pictures showing the growth of the young church. The second lesson and the Gospel for the day are both centered on that New Testament word *agape,* or Christian love.

## THE SPREADING FLAME
## ACTS 11:19-30

The post-Easter lectionary began with three scenes in Jerusalem, showing how the apostolic preaching lit some fires among Jewish believers there (the Second, Third, and Fourth Sundays of Easter). Last week the story was told about the Ethiopian official who became a believer while on the way to his African homeland. Now we have another scene, this time in the great world city of Antioch in Syria, more than three hundred miles north of Jerusalem. These lectionary texts do not provide a complete study of the book of Acts. They do, however, offer scenes that tell the story of that spreading flame.

"The blood of the martyrs was the seed of the church" is the old saying. The story of the stoning of Stephen as told in Acts 7 provides an illustration. What started out as curiosity develops into more and more intense criticism and eventually erupts into mob murder. The young church in Jerusalem experiences persecution, and the believers scatter through Judea and Samaria in fulfillment of Acts 1:8 (cf. 8:1). The seeds of the church begin to take root.

Antioch in Syria was the third largest city of the Mediterranean world, ranking after Rome and Alexandria. A pattern is emerging: after taking root in Jerusalem, the church begins to sprout up in the cities of the Mediterranean world. Paul's letters bear the names of the great cities of the day: Rome, Corinth, Ephesus. Another aspect to the pattern is that the good news is always brought first to the local synagogue (11:19).

Now, with this text, comes a decisive moment in the spread of the Christian faith. The good news is brought to non-Jews, and these Greeks begin to worship the Lord (vv. 20-21). Acts has already told the story of Cornelius, the first Gentile convert (10:1—11:18). Just as the author has reported the increasing number of Jews who believed the good news (2:41; 4:4; 5:14; 6:7), so now we hear about the influx of non-Jews into the community (11:21, 24).

Barnabas is one of the more interesting figures in the book of Acts. Saul/Paul once identified himself as a member of the tribe of Benjamin (Phil. 3:5). Barnabas is identified as a member of the tribe of Levi, which provided priests and assistants to the priests in the running of the temple (Acts 4:36; cf. Luke 10:32; John 1:19). From the island of Cyprus, he was originally named Joseph but was given the name Barnabas, understood as "son of encouragement," by the disciples. Barnabas appears to be a man with great diplomatic gifts. When Saul the former persecutor was greeted with suspicion in Jerusalem, it was Barnabas who smoothed the way for him (Acts 9:26-27). When word got to Jerusalem that non-Jews were joining the believers to the north in Antioch, it was Barnabas whom they sent to investigate the matter (Acts 11:22). This "good man, full of the Holy Spirit and of faith" (11:24), saw in the events in Antioch the hand of God. Some time earlier Saul had been sent out of Jerusalem and off to Tarsus to save his life (Acts 9:29-30). It is Barnabas who gets Saul and brings him to this great Syrian city, where they work together for a year. And here in Antioch, believers are for the first time called "Christians," which means "Messiahists," or those who believe in Jesus as Messiah. When Saul/Paul set out on his first missionary trip, it was Barnabas and his cousin John Mark who went along (Acts 13:2, 5).

The section from Acts ends with a reminder that from the very beginning, these people called "Christians" were marked by a practical concern for one another. There was a food shortage in Judea, hundreds of miles away; interestingly, that shortage had been predicted by a prophet. Luke anchors the event in history, referring to emperor Claudius (A.D. 41–54). So the first Christian "food shelf" was organized. People brought what they could. We get the impression it was done quickly. And who took the relief to the Judean Christians? Saul, who already is appearing as one of the great travelers of all time, and that "good man, full of the Holy Spirit and of faith," Barnabas.

What might the preacher want to point out from this text? First, God can work through the events of history to accomplish God's purposes. The first believers in the good news were no longer safe in Jerusalem. When they scattered about the Mediterranean world, they took the good news with them. Second, from the beginning, the early community of Christians has been open to the peoples of the world. Christianity grew out of Judaism. But we cannot read very far in Acts without sensing the openness of this faith to the other people of the world. Here it is the Greeks. Eventually the good news will spread to the ends of the earth (Acts 1:8). The story of the young church in Acts stands as a reminder that the church today is called to the same kind of hospitable welcoming of the strangers of the world. Third, as Christians, our name reminds us who we are. We are those who believe Jesus of Nazareth to be the Messiah or, in Greek, the Christ. This sets us apart from the other religions of the world. Finally, our people have a long tradition of running food shelves and doing relief work. Acts 2:43-47 gives us another picture of our earliest brothers and sisters in Christ, asking that we look at ourselves periodically to be sure that there is still a family resemblance.

# IT'S ABOUT LOVE
## 1 JOHN 4:1-11

The lectionary takes us on a continuing investigation of this central section of 1 John. A week ago, we identified 1 John 3:23 as summarizing what the Christian life is all about.

According to that text: (1) It is about believing in Jesus Christ and (2) it is about loving one another. In the text for today, the author continues to play upon those two themes. 1 John 4:1-6 speaks about believing in Jesus Christ, and vv. 7-11 are about loving one another. The lectionary cuts the text with v. 11; since the lesson for the Seventh Sunday of Easter picks up with v. 13, and since v. 12 rounds off the paragraph, there would seem to be no reason to neglect v. 12.

Wedding sermons, when the topic is love, often select 1 Corinthians 13 as the text. The sections of 1 John assigned to this Sunday and the next (4:13-21) are equally noteworthy texts that speak of Christian love.

Today's text divides quite clearly into three sections, each introduced by the word "Beloved" (Greek, *agapētoi*): 4:1-6, 7-10, 11-12. Except for that initial "beloved," vv. 1-6 do not mention the word "love" or any of its cognates; in vv. 7-12, however, a form of the Greek *agapē* comes up some fifteen times. This "love" theme will continue in 4:13-21 for next week. Both texts have the statement, "God is love" (4:8, 16).

The entire discussion in 1 John 4 should be seen in connection with the theme sounded in 3:23: "And this is his commandment, that we should believe in the name of his Son Jesus Christ and love one another, just as he has commanded us."

The author has just said that we can tell whether Jesus Christ lives in us by the Spirit that has been given to us. Now, with today's text, the writer picks up on that word, "Spirit."

"Beloved, do not believe every spirit . . ." is the theme for 4:1-6. Here is the negative side of the positive commandment given in 3:23. We should like to know more about the "false prophets" (literally "pseudo-prophets") that the author targets here. The whole paragraph is concerned with right teaching. Some "prophets" going about the church are phonies, pseudos, false. They propagate "the spirit of error" (v. 6). The word translated "error" here is *planē* with the literal sense, "wandering, roaming about." A "planet" is a heavenly body that does not march through the night sky in formation with the stars; it is a wanderer, off on its own, making its own way. The "spirit of error" (*planē*) is thus a spirit enticing its followers to march to their own drummer, to get out of step and to drop out of rank with the people of God. Verse 2 gives us a hint as to what these off-course pseudo-prophets taught, or rather what they failed to teach. They denied that Jesus Christ had come in the flesh. He only "seemed" to be human (see the comments in connection with 1 John 5 for the Second Sunday of Easter).

Let it be noted that the writer of 1 John does not simply call members of the early Christian community to love one another, important as that was and is. Before speaking about how Christians ought to act toward one another, he speaks about Jesus Christ (3:23), and in fact about Jesus Christ rightly understood (4:2-3). Authentic Christian ethics grows out of right Christology.

"Beloved, let us love one another" introduces 4:7-10. Here is that great Christian word, *agapē*, found also in John 3:16, 1 Corinthians 13, and throughout the New Testament. What about love in the Christian faith? A few things are expressed with crystal clarity in these few verses: (1) This sort of love originates in the heart of God. Here is that Bible verse, "God is love," that the children still learn and that we continue to try to understand. Whatever the sort of love described in the New Testament looks like, its origin is clear. It comes from God who in some way *is* love. (2) This sort of love came into the world in a unique way through God's Son, who paid the price for our sins (vv. 9-10). (3) This sort of love gives us the gift of life (v. 9). A love that frees us from sin and sets us free to live—so this loving and living is here pictured.

"Beloved, since God loved us so much, we also ought to love one another" (4:11). The same thing will be said in 4:19, identifying the source of our love for God and for one another as the love of God in Christ that we have already experienced: "We love because he first loved us." Of course this is nothing new. The Old Testament directives indicating how we ought to relate to God and to others grow out of the reminder that this is the God who "brought you out of the land of Egypt" (Exodus 20; Deuteronomy 5).

1 John, like the Gospel of John, has a way of infusing new content into old words: "God is light . . . God is love" (1:5, 4:8, 16). What is the Christian faith all about? For one thing, it is about love—love in that shape of "because he first loved us, we love." For another thing, it is about life.

As I read this text I cannot help but hear the words of an old camp song that sang about both love and life:

> *Lovin's really livin',*
> > *without it, you ain't livin', boy,*
> *you're just getting up each day and walkin' 'round.*

The author of 1 John, I'm confident, would agree.

## IT'S ABOUT LOVE (CONTINUED)
## JOHN 15:9-17

The setting for these words of Jesus was discussed in connection with last week's Gospel text. For this week, the lectionary puts the spotlight on the second part of Jesus' words about the vine and the branches. The picture continues, as the charge to "bear fruit" in v. 16 indicates, but now the emphasis is different. If the focus in vv. 1-8 was on the relationship between Christ and believers under the figure of vine and branches, the emphasis is now on relationships among believers. In this connection one of the great New Testament words is introduced: the verb *agapao* and the noun *agapē*, translated as "love." As further commentary, the lectionary points us to 1 John 4:1-11. Since no other Sunday emphasizes the matter of *agapē* to this degree, we shall want to sharpen up our understanding of this central New Testament term.

A glance at the occurrences of this key word in this text indicates that it is used here in connection with three relationships; verbs are italicized:

1. Love of God the Father for Jesus the Son (9, 10).
2. Love of Jesus for the disciples: "you" (9, 9, 10, 12); "friends" (*13*).
3. Love of the disciples for one another (*12*, *17*).

Consideration of the use of the noun and verb in this text indicates a pattern. This love is first described as from the Father to Jesus; a similar kind of love is relayed from Jesus to the disciples; the disciples are encouraged to remain in that love (we shall ask just what this means) as Jesus remains in the Father's love (vv. 9-10).

But this is more than just a relationship between Father and Son or Son and disciples. The section in vv. 12-17 is framed by references to the third type of love as indicated above, love among the disciples themselves. Type 3, however, is seen as modeled on type 2, which is modeled on type 1. To summarize: (1) The Father loves Jesus. (2) Jesus loves the disciples in that same way. (3) The disciples ought to love one another in this way. This *agapē* is thus described as flowing from Father to Son to disciples and then back and forth to one another.

The text falls into two sections, which we might title by picking up the imperatives at the beginning of each: remain in my love (vv. 9-11) and love one another (vv. 12-17).

What does "abide in my love" mean? The clue is provided by that branch broken from a birch tree, as mentioned in last week's comments on John 15. A "believer" not rightly related to Jesus is like a branch no longer in touch with the vine. Such an existence can bear no fruit and is in fact in danger of destruction (15:4-6). To "abide in my love" sharpens the focus of "abide in me." It means a life patterned on that of Jesus Christ. Just as Jesus kept his Father's commandments and thus remained in touch with that source of *agapē*, so Jesus' disciples ought to keep his commandments. Does this mean an existence constantly fretting, observing this regulation or keeping that rule? The next words of Jesus hardly point in this direction. Such a life is marked by joy, merriment, and hilarity. Whatever "keeping his commandments" means, it clearly cannot be an uptight, calculating religion of rule-keeping.

Verses 12-17 shed more insight on the question. If "abide in my love" means observing commandments, here that kind of life is described. In fact, far from fussing over pious prescriptions or religious regulations, Jesus boils commandment-keeping down to one: "This is my commandment, that you love one another" (v. 12). What will that love look like? "You have had an example in the last years we have been together," Jesus is saying. "Show the same kind of love to each other that I have shown to you." And then, in the charged atmosphere of the last evening before the events leading up to the cross, Jesus cites a saying with an ominous ring: "No one has greater love than this, to lay down one's life for one's friends." We who know the rest of the story understand what that means.

How ought we to understand our relationship to Jesus? Texts over the past weeks have given us a picture of a shepherd and sheep (Fourth Sunday of Easter), of a vine and branches (Fifth Sunday of Easter), and now we have another picture. We—that is, believers—are described as "friends" of Jesus. A few observations on this description: First, to be a friend is more than to be a servant. In this intimate setting just before the end events, Jesus is intending to describe a relationship that has changed. Earlier he had referred to the disciples as servants (13:16; also 12:26). Now he calls them friends. Second, to be a friend means to be in on some private knowledge about the other. Servants are here defined as those who do not get in on private discussions in the master's house. In this case, Jesus calls the disciples friends, saying that he has let these friends in on *everything* that he has heard from his Father. Such a label is quite rare in the Old Testament. Abraham was called "friend of God" (Isa. 41:8; 2 Chron. 20:7; James 2:23; cf. Wisd. of Sol, 7:27). Third, the language here speaks only of believers as friends of Jesus. Nothing is said about Jesus as "friend." The emphasis here is not on an easy familiarity or equality; v. 16 makes that clear. The lines from hymns, "What a Friend We Have in Jesus" or "Friend of sinners was his name" (from "One There Is, above All Others") capture another part of the New Testament tradition, where Jesus is called "a friend of tax collectors and sinners" (Matt. 11:19; Luke 7:34).

Verse 16 indicates that the initiative for this relationship came from Jesus. This text illustrates the biblical theme that being chosen always means being chosen for a purpose. That purpose is described as Jesus returns to the theme introduced at the beginning: the disciples have been chosen in order to "bear fruit"; see also Gal. 5:22-23. Jesus returns to the theme of prayer (v. 7), indicating that prayer ought to be "in my name." The whole discussion of *agapē* ends with a repeat of the command to love one another.

# The Ascension of Our Lord

| Lutheran | Roman Catholic | Episcopal | Common Lectionary |
|----------|----------------|-----------|-------------------|
| Acts 1:1-11 | Acts 1:1-11 | Acts 1:1-11 | Acts 1:1-11 |
| Eph. 1:16-23 | Eph. 1:17-23 | Eph. 1:15-23 | Eph. 1:15-23 |
| Luke 24:44-53 | Mark 16:15-20 | Luke 24:49-53 | Luke 24:46-53 or Mark 16:9-16, 19-20 |

The three texts assigned for this day all have their focus on the ascension. Psalm 110, the psalm for the day, also has something to contribute to the understanding of this event. The most complete account of the ascension is given in Acts. The book of Luke ends with a short report, while the Ephesians text is a sample of how the New Testament views the significance of the ascension. In a sermon for Ascension Day, the preacher will probably want to take Acts 1 as the major text, with the others providing further interpretation and commentary.

## WHERE DO WE GO FROM HERE?
## ACTS 1:1-11

The lectionary insists that the ascension be understood in its broader context. The text may be divided as follows: 1:1-2: the connection with Luke's Gospel; vv. 3-5: the further appearances of Jesus; vv. 6-8: the last words of Jesus to his disciples; vv. 9-11: the ascension.

The "first book" of 1:1 is Luke's Gospel, also dedicated to this person named Theophilus (cf. Luke 1:3). That book covered the period from the beginning of the Jesus story through the ascension.

According to Acts, the forty days after Easter were marked by actions which demonstrated that Jesus had indeed arisen from the dead, and by teaching concerning the kingdom of God. What might have been the content of that teaching? Luke provides a clue at the end of his Gospel. Jesus took his two companions on the road to Emmaus on a walk through the Old Testament, showing them that the Messiah (popularly conceived as a political super-king) had to suffer in order to accomplish his mission (Luke 24:25-27). Jesus conducted the same sort of Bible study for the disciples gathered in Jerusalem (Luke 24:44-49). At that time he told them to wait in Jerusalem until they were "clothed with power from on high" (24:49). That same order is now given again, more than a month later. "Stay in Jerusalem . . . John baptized with water, but you will receive a baptism with the Holy Spirit, and in just a few days," says Jesus.

Acts 1:6-8 offers Luke's account of the last words of Jesus. Jesus had been going through the Hebrew Scriptures with the disciples, giving them a Bible study on the kingdom of God (1:3). Central to that kingdom, as we see from Luke 24:26 and 46, was the notion that the Messiah would accomplish his mission through suffering. This certainly was contrary to popular Jewish expectations connected with the Messiah, conceived as one who would rule all nations, rule forever, and put all enemies under his feet (e.g., Psalms 2, 72, 110; Isaiah 7, 9, 11). Jesus was talking about establishing something other than a political kingdom. But v. 6 shows that the disciples had a hard time getting that straight. They said: "But Lord . . . *now* will you do it? Now will you make us a powerful nation once again? Now will you put Israel on the map again, like it was during the time of David?" After all, Jesus was to rule on the throne of David (Luke 1:32).

Jesus replies to the question with a negative and a positive word. You can't know all the secrets of your heavenly Father, he says (v. 7). But you do have a promise (and here are the last words of Jesus to his closest friends): The Holy Spirit will come upon you. You will receive *power* (a word associated with the receiving of the Holy Spirit in Acts; see 1:8 and the discussion of 2:1-21 in The Day of Pentecost below). Then Luke indicates the plan for this book. It will record the telling of the story about Jesus in Jerusalem (chaps. 1–7), in Judea and Samaria (chaps. 8–12), and to the ends of the earth (chaps. 13–28).

This opening of the book of Acts thus does two things. It links up the present activities of the apostles, now gathered in Jerusalem, to the past (Acts 1:1-5). More important, it points to their work for the future, when they will receive power and will witness to the ends of the earth (1:8).

And then what happens? There is some confusion in the way in which Jesus' leaving the earth is remembered. According to Luke 24:50-51, Jesus lifted up his hands, pronounced a blessing, and was taken into heaven, like an Old Testament prophet (2 Kings 2:9-12). The longer ending of Mark remembers his exit the same way, adding that he "sat down at the right hand of God" (Mark 16:19). In this account, Jesus is lifted up, a cloud covers him, and he is gone (Acts 1:9).

The accounts of Jesus' resurrection tell in detail the events of his death, including his burial in the tomb. Next they pick up the story after Jesus has been raised from the dead. There are no descriptions of the actual event of the dead Jesus coming back to a new kind of life. We have no videotape-like report of what happened in the tomb.

What happened to Jesus after the resurrection? He was around for a while, though the New Testament accounts disagree on exactly how long, but very soon he was in heaven. The writers use metaphorical language, describing him as sitting "at the right hand of God" (Mark 16:19; Eph. 1:20; Heb. 1:3; 8:1; 10:12; 12:2; the Apostles' Creed). His postresurrection appearances are described and his present residence with God is declared. There is considerable reticence in the text when it comes to describing just how he got from earth to heaven. Mark 16:19 simply says he was "taken up." Luke 24:51 says he was "carried up," and this account of Acts 1:9 says he was lifted up and taken away by a cloud. As is the case with the resurrection accounts, the narrative tells of his preascension appearances, then of his residence with the Father in heaven, but does not dwell on how Jesus got from one place to the other. In fact, the whole event is shrouded in a cloud! The disciples must have wondered: Where do we go from here? One thing is certain: Jesus still lives and is still active. Stephen sees him at the right hand of God (Acts 7:55-56). Saul will soon encounter the risen Christ and a whole new chapter in the story of the young church will begin (Acts 9).

In the meantime, says Jesus, "Wait."

## WHERE IS CHRIST NOW?
## EPHESIANS 1:16-23

Sunday after Sunday, in a great variety of languages, believers around the world confess, "He ascended into heaven, and is seated at the right hand of the Father." This two-part confession first tells of the ascension and then speaks of the risen Christ's present position. Acts 1 reports the ascension, while our Ephesians text helps to understand that second statement in the Apostles' Creed.

After the standard opening for a letter in 1:1-2, the Greek of Ephesians starts off with two unusually long sentences: 1:3-14 and 15-23. Modern translations break these up for clarity, as do some editions of the Greek New Testament. The first sentence is praise of God: "Praise be to the God and father of our Lord Jesus Christ" (1:3 NIV). The second is a prayer of thanksgiving: "For this reason, ever since I heard about your faith in the Lord Jesus and your love for all the saints, I have not stopped giving thanks for you. . ." (1:15 NIV). With v. 17, the prayer begins. The lectionary text for today is thus a part of this prayer at the beginning of the letter to the Ephesians.

This letter gives us an insight into the importance of prayer in the life of these early Christians. Paul is accustomed to praying for this young congregation (1:16) and ends his letter by urging them to pray for one another and for him in prison, as he awaits trial (6:18-20).

The first part of the prayer asks that God give these new Christians wisdom so that they can understand two things: the hope that they have for a future inheritance, and God's power (vv. 17-19).

These letters are written to people who have already heard the good news about what God has done in Jesus Christ. Therefore Paul does not spell out that gospel, but assumes it and occasionally alludes to it. Note the way in which v. 20 speaks of the resurrection: God is the subject of the action. God raised Christ and has now "seated him at his right hand in the heavenly places." What does this "seated . . . at his right hand" mean?

The background to the expression is to be found in Psalm 110. Translating the divine name as "Yahweh," it reads:

Yahweh said to my lord [i.e., to my king],
   "Sit at my right hand
until I make your enemies your footstool."

This is one of the royal psalms, used as part of the liturgy for installing a new king in Jerusalem. The new king is described as seated at the right hand of Yahweh. To be "at the right hand" means to occupy the place of honor; Psalm 45 describes a royal wedding, with the queen standing at the right of the king (v. 10). The sense survives in the expression "right-hand man," that is, one's most trusted assistant. Thus when the king is installed, he is described as God's "right-hand man."

These psalms used at events in the life of the monarch describe the king in extravagant language. They pray that he might live forever (Ps. 72:5), that he might conquer all nations (72:9-11; 2:8-9), bring righteousness and peace (72:7), and rule over the entire world (72:8). He is called the Lord's anointed or, in Hebrew, Messiah (2:2; 45:7). He is installed on Mount Zion by God himself and addressed as son of God (2:6-7). Taken together, these royal psalms set forth an ideal description for each new king: one who would rule forever, rule the entire world, establish justice, bring peace, and who would indeed be the Lord's right-hand man. But king after king was a disappointment, so that this extravagant language becomes more and more a projection of hopes for a super-king, an anointed one or messiah, who would appear in the future. The New Testament sees Jesus as that long-awaited Messiah and claims these titles for him. When Eph. 1:20 speaks of Christ (Hebrew, *Messiah*) seated at the right hand of God in heaven, this is language right out of the tradition of these royal psalms. This phrase from Psalm 110 permeates the New Testament and must have been very important in the earliest interpretations of Jesus as Messiah (Mark 16:19; Acts 2:34; Heb. 1:3; 8:1; 10:12; 12:2).

The Gospel text for this Sunday makes brief mention of the ascension. The text from Acts provides some description of the event. This letter to the Ephesians speaks of God raising Christ from the dead and then immediately focuses on Christ's position in heaven, at God's right hand.

What is the risen Christ doing now? He is seated at God's right hand in heaven, which means he occupies a position of honor and power. Verse 21 indicates that the risen Christ is high above any other authority or power that exists anywhere (in space) or that will exist in the future (in time).

Verse 22 uses the language of Ps. 8:6 to express the rule of the risen Christ. Then Paul shifts into one of the great pictures of the church in the Pauline literature: the church is Christ's body, the risen Christ the head.

The key point of contact here is the expression "seated at the right hand of the Father." Every Christian knows those words from the Creed. The occurrence of this text in the lectionary provides the occasion to explain just what that means.

# WHAT DO WE DO NEXT?
## LUKE 24:44-53

The Gospel of Luke has been characterized as a Gospel of joy. It begins with a scene in the temple, when an angel appears to aging Zechariah and tells him that his wife will give birth to a child, and "You will have joy and gladness, and many will rejoice at his birth" (1:14). In the middle of the book are the three parables of the lost, each concluding with a joyful celebration (chap. 15). And now Luke's Gospel ends as it began, showing us a scene in the temple, where there are people worshiping "with great joy" (24:52).

Luke's Gospel ends with Jesus leaving his disciples. Then how can it conclude on this note of joy?

Luke 24, it will be recalled, presents three postresurrection scenes, all taking place on that first Easter Sunday. The setting for the first is the empty tomb (vv. 1-12), for the second the road to Emmaus (vv. 13-35), and for the third a room where the disciples are gathered in Jerusalem (vv. 36-49). The second and third scenes made up the Gospel text for the Third Sunday of Easter. With this week's text, the lectionary overlaps a part of the third scene in the Jerusalem room (vv. 36-49) and then presents the conclusion of Luke's Gospel, first at Bethany (v. 50-51) and then in the Jerusalem temple (vv. 52-53).

Verses 44-49 should be considered in connection with vv. 36-43. Together they give us a report on the events on the evening of the first Easter Sunday. The focus in 36-43 is on certain acts of Jesus. He suddenly appears, greets his friends with the usual "Shalom," invites them to "touch and see" that he is a real person and not a ghost, and then eats fish with them.

The focus in vv. 44-49 is on Jesus' words, in fact his last words, according to Luke's Gospel. This is an important section that looks back at the time "while I was still with you" and then looks forward to a telling of all the story about Jesus "to all nations." What should the disciples do next? Just wait in this city, says Jesus, "until you have been clothed with power from on high." This directive and promise of Jesus explains why these closest friends of his can be joyful, even after Jesus has left them. They have something to look forward to. They will receive some sort of power (Greek, *dynamis*) from "on high," that is, from God the Father.

Verses 50-53 provide snapshots of two scenes. The first is Jesus' ascension into heaven (vv. 50-51) and the second is a scene in the temple (vv. 52-53). Only two of the Gospels report the ascension of Jesus; in addition to Luke, the longer ending of Mark has a brief comment (Mark 16:19). Verse 51 appears to stand in tension with the longer account of the ascension in Acts 1:1-11. Here it appears that Jesus ascended on the evening of Easter; in Acts 1, the ascension takes place after forty days. This tension was felt by early copyists, who eliminated the words "and was carried up into heaven" (NRSV footnote). Because Acts 1:2 assumes that the Gospel tells of the ascension, and because of manuscript evidence, the NRSV text retains this brief mention of Jesus' departure. Luke has another account of Jesus simply vanishing (24:31); here he seems to offer a telescoped version of the events.

Bethany is a village a mile and a half out of Jerusalem, on the eastern slope of the Mount of Olives. Jesus raises his hands in a typical gesture of blessing. Sirach 50:20 says: "Then Simon came down and raised his hands over the whole congregation of Israelites, to pronounce the blessing of the Lord with his lips. . . ." Leviticus 9:22 reports the same gesture: "Aaron lifted his hands toward the people and blessed them. . . ." Jesus is portrayed here as a priest. Just as a pastor pronounces a blessing at the end of a worship service, so Jesus blesses his closest friends.

Luke 24:31 had said that Jesus simply vanished. Here in 24:51 it is said that he "was carried up into heaven." Acts 1 will give an expanded account of this departure.

The preacher should not miss the note of anticipation and of joy as Luke's Gospel ends. What would these disciples now do? The answer is simple. They worshiped this risen Jesus, whom they knew to be the Messiah. They were often in the temple praising God for what had happened. And they remembered the promise of the Father: soon they would receive power from on high.

Life will go on, even after Jesus no longer walks among them. They have that promise. And so this Ascension Day looks forward to the day of Pentecost, when the promise will be fulfilled.

# Seventh Sunday of Easter

| Lutheran | Roman Catholic | Episcopal | Common Lectionary |
|---|---|---|---|
| Acts 1:15-26 | Acts 1:15-17, 20a, 20c-26 | Acts 1:15-26 | Acts 1:15-17, 21-26 |
| 1 John 4:13-21 | 1 John 4:11-16 | 1 John 5:9-15 | 1 John 5:9-13 |
| John 17:11b-19 | John 17:11b-19 | John 17:11b-19 | John 17:11b-19 |

The reading from Acts is assigned to this Sunday because it presents a scene from the life of the early church in the period between the ascension and Pentecost. The final selection in the series of readings from 1 John is once again about the nature of Christian love. The Gospel offers the third in a series of texts taken from the words of Jesus to his disciples just before the events leading up to the crucifixion.

## AND THEN THERE WERE TWELVE
## ACTS 1:15-26

*15-17.* The older versions translated the Greek literally as "brethren" in vv. 15 and 16; NRSV translates as "believers" and "friends" (see the footnotes), assuming the presence of women in the group (see 1:14).

One of the convictions of the earliest preachers in Acts is that the promises of the Old Testament Scriptures are being fulfilled and that events are taking place according to God's plans (e.g., 2:16-21, 23; 3:18, 24-25; 4:11; 10:43; 13:32-37). Peter now interprets the defection of Judas in the light of those convictions. Even this betrayal was a fulfillment of Scripture!

*18-20.* Peter did not include these words in his speech. He is in Jerusalem and everybody living there knows what happened to Judas (v. 19). Luke supplies this information for those who will read the account later.

Luke's Gospel had said nothing further about Judas after reporting his role in the betrayal of Jesus (Luke 22:47-53). Those who read Acts or hear it read are now told what happened to Judas, and also how his replacement was chosen. With the money he received for betraying Jesus, Judas had bought a piece of land. According to the story as Luke picked it up, Judas apparently fell from a roof or from some other high place and died. Since he "burst open," the field was called in Aramaic *Hakeldama*, translated here as "Field of Blood" (Greek, *chōrion haimatos*).

Mark had reported how Judas identified Jesus with a kiss, then said nothing more about the fate of Judas (Mark 14:43-45). Of course, everyone would have been curious: What happened to that betrayer? Writing after Mark,

Matthew gives a full account. After the betrayal, Judas was remorseful, tried unsuccessfully to return the money, and then hanged himself. The money was used to buy the field where he was buried (here the stories overlap) and the field was called "Field of Blood" (Greek, *agros haimatos*, another translation of the Aramaic *Hakeldama*). The two accounts agree on the fact of Judas's death and the place of death; Luke's sources (Luke 1:1-3) reported a version of the details of the death that was different from the one given by Matthew.

Verse 20 returns to the words of Peter's speech. The Judas events, says the apostle, are the fulfillment of two Old Testament texts. Among a series of curses on enemies in Ps. 69:22-28 are the words, "May their camp be a desolation"; Peter assumes the text of the Greek Old Testament here, which explains the variation from the NRSV translation of the words of the psalm.

Psalm 109 also presents a series of curses against enemies. Among them are the words, "May his days be few; may another seize his position" (v. 8), again quoted here (Acts 1:20) from the Greek Old Testament.

Even the matter involving Judas, Peter is saying, is a fulfillment of Scripture.

*21-26.* Peter suggests two requirements for the one who will replace Judas: That person must have been with the disciples since the beginning, the time of Jesus' baptism, and that person must be one who had seen Jesus after the resurrection. Here is a reminder that the Bible does not tell us everything about the events of Jesus' ministry and does not name every person who knew Jesus.

Two candidates, Barsabbas and Matthias, are suggested. How should the decision be made? A two-step process is employed, involving prayer and then the casting of lots, the ancient equivalent of drawing straws, most likely using small stones or sticks. The same language is used in describing the casting of lots on the ship where Jonah is passenger (Jon. 1:7). Prayer and the casting of lots was seen as the way in which the Lord revealed his will (see Prov. 16:33). Matthias gets the long straw and once again there are twelve apostles. We hear nothing more of either of these two.

A final comment on this incident, reported after the ascension and before Pentecost: Why was it so important that Judas be replaced? We find a clue in Luke 22:28-30. There were twelve tribes in Israel (Genesis 49) and, says Luke, there will be twelve thrones in the future kingdom of God. The twelve disciples will sit on those twelve thrones, therefore the number twelve must be maintained. There is continuity between the new people of God being formed and the ancient twelve-tribe people of Israel.

## WHAT DOES CHRISTIAN LOVE LOOK LIKE?
## 1 JOHN 4:13-21

This Sunday presents the sixth and final text in the series taken from 1 John. There is no question as to the central theme of this section of this letter: once again, it is about love. Forms of the Greek verb *agapao* (to love) or the noun *agapē* (love) occur 14 times in this short section. This section is not just about love in general, but about love that is specifically Christian. Few passages in the Bible bring Christian love into focus with the clarity that we find here.

*13-16a.* John's way of expressing the believer's relationship to God and God's relationship to the believer is to use the Greek verb *menō*, which means "remain, abide." When we obey God's commandments, John has said, we abide in him, and God abides in us and gives us his Spirit (1 John 3:24). This same thought introduces today's pericope selection. These initial verses provide a good example of the way in which the Christian teaching of the Trinity informs the writings of the New Testament. *God* has sent God's *Son as Savior* and has given to us a measure of God's *Spirit* (vv. 13-14). Once again, in the face of certain heretical views floating around, Christians are those who make a confession (v. 15; also 4:2), specifically a confession that Jesus is the Son of God.

John is about to begin a discourse on the shape of Christian love. The first thing he speaks about here is "the love that God has for us" (v. 16).

*16b-21.* This biblical author does not develop a theme step-by-step, in outline form, but rather keeps returning to a few major themes, stating them and then restating them. This paragraph begins with the statement already made in 4:8: "God is love."

Verse 19 puts the matter clearly and succinctly: We love because he first loved us. Some later copyists thought that this was not sufficiently clear and therefore added "God," while still others supplied the object, "We love him" (see the NRSV notes).

Verses 20 and 21 represent a special concern of the author. Apparently there were those in the congregation who declared, "I love God" but who did not couple this love of God with concern for their brothers and sisters in the community of believers. Once again, John is using family language to describe the relationship of those in the Christian community (see the comments on 3:1-2 for the Fourth Sunday of Easter). The matter is clear. One cannot just mouth pious phrases like "I love God" and on that basis consider oneself a Christian. Christianity is more than talk. Those who love God are also expected to show concern for the other members of their family of faith.

Let us then summarize by noting the shape of Christian loving, as sketched in these verses. We could imagine a diagram on a blackboard or on a piece of paper. At the top of the diagram is the word *God*, who is the source of love (4:8, 16). That love (represented with a vertical line) came down from heaven in the person of Jesus Christ, whose death for our sins was the expression of God's love for us (4:14-16, 9-10). God first loved us, and therefore we ought to be motivated to love God in return—and also to show love (represented with a horizontal line) to our brothers and sisters (4:19-20, 11).

In sum, the shape of Christian love as here described is as follows: God's love came down from heaven to earth in Jesus Christ, is reflected back in love to God and also in love to brothers and sisters. Not surprisingly, the movement of love from God to us and from us to our siblings turns out to take the shape of a cross.

## WORLDLY CHRISTIANS
## JOHN 17:11b-19

If you have a Bible that prints the words of Jesus in red, you notice a lot of red in John 14–17! These chapters are almost exclusively words from Jesus himself (as presented by John, of course) and are therefore among the most treasured parts of Scripture. The Gospel texts for the past two Sundays showed Jesus teaching, describing himself as a vine and his followers as branches. In this text we hear Jesus praying—in fact, we have the longest recorded prayer of Jesus.

The prayer in John 17 falls into three divisions, linked by a logical progression. First, Jesus prays for himself (vv. 1-5), then he prays for his disciples (vv. 6-19), and finally he prays for those who will believe in the future (vv. 20-26). This Sunday's text comes from the middle section of this prayer.

After commenting on the movement of the text as a whole, we shall focus briefly on three themes that stand out in this passage: the world, the word, and the oneness of the church.

*11b-12.* The address "Holy Father" is found only here (11b) in John's Gospel. "Father" is, of course, a term appropriately expressing Jesus' close relationship to God. Jesus uses it frequently in this prayer (17:1, 5, 11, 21, 24, 25). The basic sense of "holy" is "separate, other," here expressing the otherness of God (see also Isa. 6:1-5; Hos. 11:1-9). The combination of the two words thus expresses both the dimensions of closeness (Father/Son) and transcendence (holy). These same dimensions of intimacy and distance occur in Matt. 11:25-27, where Jesus addresses God as "Father, Lord of heaven and earth."

Jesus asks that God "protect" these eleven disciples, just as Jesus himself had protected them while he was with them. The sense of the Greek word is to "keep" or "guard," just as one guards or keeps watch over prisoners in a jail (Acts 12:6; 16:23). The word "guarded" is also used for watching over possessions so that they are not stolen (Acts 22:20). Why should Jesus ask that his Father protect and guard these disciples? They are going to be living "in the world," and the world is a place where they will have to face persecution (John 16:33). Knowing what is out there for his friends in "the world," Jesus asks God to protect them.

This prayer has a way of looking toward the future and is indeed designed to include those believers who will come in the future. We have noted this same future orientation in Jesus' words about the good shepherd (John 10:16). Jesus seems to be anticipating divisions in the future church (see 1 Corinthians 1, for example) and thus prays that God will somehow hold these believers together, "so that they may be one." He compares that oneness to the mysterious oneness between himself and the Father. That prayer for oneness is again sounded in 17:20-21.

Verse 12 refers to Judas, who has betrayed Jesus (13:18-30). Jesus had announced earlier that Scripture foretold the fact that one would betray him (13:18; quoting Ps. 41:9). Verses 13-19 speak about the continuing life of the disciples in the world. Jesus is leaving the world (v. 11) but they will stay behind.

This is a quite realistic picture of Christian existence in the world. It will not all be sweetness and roses! "In the world you face persecution" (John 16:33), Jesus had said earlier. In fact, believers can expect that the people of the world will hate them (17:14).

So what should the disciples—and those who will become believers because of them—do in the world? Here is no call to flee the world, like the famed fifth-century A.D. pole-sitter Simeon Stylites, who sat on the top of a column more than 150 feet high for nearly forty years, succeeding at least in getting 150 feet away from the world.

These disciples have a model in how Jesus lived. God sent him into the world (v. 17; 3:16), and now Jesus is sending them into the world. The older translations spoke of being "in the world but not of it"; "they are not of the world, even as I am not of the world" (v. 16, RSV).

So these followers of Jesus are sent right into the midst of the world, with all its aches and pains, aggravations, and persecutions. Even though they will live in the world, their true residence is somewhere else. Jesus had said, "I go to prepare a place for you" (14:2). In the meantime, however, they are to plunge into the life of the world of their own day with all the vigor and engagement that Jesus showed in his own life.

These believers are sustained by two things. Jesus prayed for them, asking that his heavenly Father protect them from the evil one. And they have God's word, as found in the Old Testament Scriptures now being fulfilled, and also in the person of Jesus (1:14) and now in this Gospel, written "that through believing you may have life in his name" (20:31).

Though not of the world, these Christians are nevertheless called to live in the world. The writer of Hebrews expressed the same ideas in different language. He spoke of our ancestors in the faith as a wandering people of God, "strangers and foreigners on the earth" (Heb. 11:13) who lived in tents but who were always looking forward to "the city that has foundations, whose architect and builder is God" (11:10).

The writer of 1 Peter addresses fellow believers as "exiles," that is, as people who are not living in their homeland. While Christians are here on earth, they are given all the magnificent titles used of their ancestors in the faith, as told about in the Old Testament. They are "a chosen race, a royal priesthood, a holy nation, God's own people." And their calling is described in terms that the writer of the Fourth Gospel would understand, "that you may proclaim the mighty acts of him who called you out of darkness into his marvelous light" (1 Pet. 2:9). Such is the task of aliens and exiles (1 Pet. 2:11), fully involved in this world with its hurts (1 Pet. 5:9), and sustained with the promise of a heavenly inheritance (1 Pet. 1:4) and a place in the Father's house, prepared by Jesus himself (John 14:1-2).

# The Day of Pentecost

| Lutheran | Roman Catholic | Episcopal | Common Lectionary |
|---|---|---|---|
| Ezek. 37:1-14 | Acts 2:1-11 | Acts 2:1-11 or Isa. 44:1-8 | Acts 2:1-11 or Ezek. 37:1-14 |
| Acts 2:1-21 | 1 Cor. 12:3b-7, 12-13 | 1 Cor. 12:4-13 or Acts 2:1-11 | Rom. 8:22-27 or Acts 2:1-21 |
| John 7:37-39a | John 20:19-23 | John 20:19-23 or 14:8-17 | John 15:26-27; 16:4b-15 |

Two of today's texts are closely associated with Jewish festivals. The Gospel tells of Jesus in Jerusalem at the time of Sukkot, or the Festival of Booths. Pentecost is still celebrated by Jews today as Shavuot, or the Feast of Weeks. The Ezekiel text presents one of the most well known visions of that Hebrew prophet. Considering these connections, this could be a good Sunday to say something about relationships between Christians and Jews.

## THEM BONES, THEM BONES, THEM DRY BONES
## EZEKIEL 37:1-14

Not many people in the pews can say much about the prophet Ezekiel. But if you start to sing a few bars of "Dry Bones," those in the pews or even on the streets will perk up with recognition. Pentecost is a good time to give that song—and this text—a context, and a hearing.

Ezekiel is something of a strange bird among the prophets. He was told to carry out such actions as lying on his side for more than a year, cooking with cow manure, shearing his head with a sword, and the like (chaps. 4–5). His visions of creatures with four faces and four wings, of coals of fire and wheels within wheels also set him apart from the others in the fellowship of the prophets. Never, one suspects, has he been among the most popular, the most read, or most understood of that company!

But thanks to that spiritual, lots of people know about the valley of the dry bones.

We encounter Ezekiel living in Babylon, having been taken there with the first group of exiles in 597 B.C. He functioned as a pastor to the Jewish people during this darkest hour of their history. In 587 B.C. Jerusalem was totally destroyed (2 Kings 25) and most of the people were deported to Babylon.

We can pick up something of the mood of those in exile from words in the Psalms and Prophets. They wondered whether worship could continue in this foreign land (Psalm 137). They thought the Lord was paying no attention to them (Isa. 42:27) and had in fact forsaken and forgotten them (Isa. 49:14). They sang sad songs, lamenting the fall of Jerusalem, the one-time princess who had now become a widow (Lamentations 1). It is this situation of depression and despair that Ezekiel is called to address.

The text assigned for this Sunday falls into two sections: the vision (37:1-10) and the interpretation of the vision (37:11-14).

*1-6.* In his vision, Ezekiel is picked up and set down in the middle of a valley filled with bones. These are human bones, such as one might find strewn across an abandoned battlefield. Bones are lying there in heaps and they are very dry because they have been there for a long time.

"Can these bones live?" the Lord asks the prophet.

How could Ezekiel answer that one? "Lord, only you know," is his reply.

Then the Lord gives Ezekiel an order. He tells him to prophesy to the bones, telling them, "Hear the word of the Lord. . . . I will cause breath to enter you."

We should pause here to note the Pentecost connection. The Hebrew word translated breath, *ruach*, may also mean spirit or even wind, as in Gen. 1:2. The Greek Old Testament has *pneuma* here, which can also mean breath, spirit, or wind (see John 3:8). Like the account in Acts 2, this is a story about the coming of the breath/spirit of the Lord and the results of that coming.

*7-10.* The prophet does as he has been told and, in his vision, sees and hears things that have captured the imagination of all who have ever heard these words read or sung. First there is a noise, a great rattling, and the bones miraculously begin to assemble into human skeletons. Then the prophet observes something equally amazing: sinews and skin join to the bones.

But there is still no life in them.

So the prophet speaks again, and the wind/spirit/breath comes. Suddenly, instead of a valley full of parched bones, a great number of people are standing there! The dead bones have come to life.

*11-14.* What could this strange vision mean? The Lord provides the answer. The dead bones stand for the people of Israel. After all, had they not been saying, "Our bones are dried up, and our hope is lost; we are cut off completely" (v. 11)? Here is a hint for preachers: One of the techniques these prophet-preachers used in addressing their people was to base their sermons on things they had heard the people saying. Second Isaiah did that (Isa. 40:27; 49:14). Ezekiel had done the same thing before (30:10) and does it here once again.

These people, in other words, had sunk into despair and were without hope. They saw themselves as goners, as dead people. But, says the prophet, the Lord isn't through with you yet! Just as those dead and dried-up bones were enlivened by the spirit sent from the Lord, so the Lord will send his spirit. He will give life and hope to the nation that has died.

In sum: We have a people who are hopeless, discouraged, confused about the future. They have lost the external supports for their religion: land and temple. They are despondent, despairing, like so many dead and dried up carcasses. "But," says the Lord, "do not give up. I will send my spirit, and you will come alive and you will be a people again."

A half a millennium later, the Spirit would come upon a handful of followers of Jesus, discouraged because Jesus was no longer with them. The Spirit would give them power to speak and to act in Jesus' name. Once again there would be a noise—this time like the noise of a windstorm—and an unforgettable sight, this time flames of fire resting on each of them.

More about that story in the next text for this day.

## EARTH, WIND AND FIRE
## ACTS 2:1-21

There were three great Jewish festivals during the time of Jesus and the apostles: Passover, celebrating the Exodus; the Feast of Weeks, which celebrated the grain harvest; and the Festival of Booths, an autumn festival recalling the wandering in the wilderness. All three are mentioned in Deuteronomy 16; vv. 16-17 indicate that attendance at all three was required. All three are still celebrated by Jews today, usually identified by their Hebrew names: Pesach or Passover, Shavuot or Weeks, associated with the giving of the Ten Commandments, and Sukkot or Booths, when Jewish families make small huts to remind them how their ancestors lived during the days of wandering in the wilderness. The Feast of Weeks became known as Pentecost (Greek, "fiftieth") because it occurred on the fiftieth day after Passover. Both Tob. 2:1 and 2 Macc. 12:31-32 mention this Jewish festival, explaining to readers that "Pentecost" is the Greek for "Festival of Weeks."

*2:1-13.* The story begins with the apostles gathered in Jerusalem. The coming of the Holy Spirit is accompanied by a dramatic sound, "like the rush of a violent wind," and a remarkable sight, tongues of fire resting on each of them. When the Spirit comes upon someone in the Bible, that coming includes a gift of power (Acts 1:8; see examples below). This empowering by the Spirit now includes the ability to speak different languages.

The narrative is therefore something of a reversal of the story of the Tower of Babel in Genesis 11. There, the Lord punished the peoples of the earth by confusing their languages and causing a massive communications breakdown; here the Lord blesses these Jews "from every nation under heaven" (2:5) by enabling them to hear what the apostles were saying in their own languages.

What they were doing was "speaking about God's deeds of power" (2:11), or "telling in our own tongues the mighty works of God" in the RSV translation. The sound of all these languages at once suggested to some that these speakers had been drinking too much (2:13)!

*14-21.* Peter has another explanation of these events, claiming that what was happening was the fulfillment of biblical prophecy. It was Joel who, speaking in the name of the Lord, promised that "in the last days . . . I will pour out my Spirit upon all flesh" (v. 17). Those present, says Peter, were seeing this promise fulfilled.

How should one preach on this text on Pentecost Sunday? The following suggestions come to mind:

1. Acts 2 does not report the birth of a new religion but rather the fulfillment of an old one. Pentecost is often labeled as "the birthday of the church." There is a certain truth to this; as a result of this preaching, some three thousand people were baptized and added to the company of believers (2:41). However, Pentecost was and still is a Jewish festival. Few texts point out more clearly that Christianity has grown out of Judaism. This day, when the number of believers dramatically leaps from a dozen to several thousand, marks the fulfillment of some old promises. The wind and the fire that are here present will soon empower others to tell the story of the mighty deeds of God, and that story will spread like a flame across the earth (1:8).

2. When the Holy Spirit is present, things happen. In his last words to the disciples, Jesus promised that the Holy Spirit would come (Acts 1:8). As one surveys what the Bible has to say about the Spirit, one is struck by the fact that where the Spirit is, there is power, and things start happening. The Spirit of the Lord came upon Gideon, and he was empowered to defeat the Midianites (Judg. 6:34—7:25). The spirit came upon Samson and he killed a lion barehanded (Judg. 14:6), or killed thirty Philistines (14:19), or even a thousand, with the jawbone of a donkey (15:14-17).

This is also true in the Book of Acts. The gift of the Spirit is now democratized, received by all who repent and are baptized (2:38). The Spirit gives power (1:8; 10:38) including the ability to work miracles (13:9) and to carry out practical tasks (6:3, 5). The Spirit is associated with speech, giving the ability to speak in foreign languages (2:4), in tongues (10:46), or to prophesy (2:17, 18; 11:28; 20:23; 21:11), or speak boldly (4:8, 31; 6:10; 13:9). The Spirit directs the work of individuals (8:29, 39; 21:4; 10:19ff.; 11:12) or of the entire church (13:1-2, 4; 20:28). The Spirit can give joy (13:52).

3. On this Pentecost day, then, we should pray for these gifts of the Spirit for our own community, empowering us to carry out our work of speaking and of acting effectively and joyfully.

4. The Psalm assigned for Pentecost is 104:25-34. This passage speaks of the Lord's work in preserving life among the nonhuman creatures of nature. They owe their existence to the creating and sustaining Spirit of the Lord (v. 30).

# THE LIFE OF THE PARTY
## JOHN 7:37-39a

The setting for this saying of Jesus is clear, and it is important for catching the sense of the text. It is "the last day of the festival," that is, "the Jewish festival of Booths" (7:2). We begin with a few words about that festival.

In biblical times, this was one of the three yearly festivals that all Jewish males attended. We have already referred to Passover and Shavuot (Weeks or Pentecost). Sukkot or Booths was the festival that remembered the years of wandering in the wilderness, when the Israelites lived in portable shacks or booths. Leviticus 23:33-36 indicates that it lasted eight days; Num. 29:12-38 prescribes the offerings for the festival. A special feature of this festival was that the celebrants ate and slept for a week in booths made of branches, camping out for a few days as a reminder of the way they lived during the days of the wandering in the wilderness (Neh. 8:13-18).

The mood was one of celebration and thanksgiving for the harvest. It was an inclusive festival, with special concern given to inviting strangers, orphans, widows, and slaves (Deut. 16:13-15).

To this day, Pesach, Shavuot, and Sukkot remain the three major Jewish festivals. A couple of quotations from *The Jewish Catalog* (edited by Richard Siegel, Michael Strassfeld, and Sharon Strassfeld [Philadelphia: The Jewish Publication Society of America, 1973]) tell us something about the celebration of Sukkot among Jews today:

> . . . the essence of Sukkot is sheer joy. People go to great lengths to make the environment and ritual aspects of the festival beautiful and joyous. (p. 126)

Central to the celebration of the festival is the building of a sukkah. The *Catalog* gives the following directions:

> Remember never to make the sukkah overly comfortable. It should shake in the wind. One last thing—once you build it, use it. Eat every meal there (including breakfast). Sleep in it if you can. Invite guests to your sukkah and share it with all who have none. (p. 130)

For Jews today, just after Sukkot comes the festival of Simhat Torah, or rejoicing with the Torah. The joyful mood continues, with people carrying the Torah scrolls in a parade around the synagogue and sometimes through the streets, accompanied by dancing and singing.

From biblical times until today, the festival of Sukkot has been a time of rejoicing and celebrating. It was among the best times, the happiest times that Judaism had to offer. What would Jesus have to say in the midst of such a celebration?

Water and rain played a big part in the celebration of the feast in Jesus' day. Zechariah 14:16-19 describes a future celebration of the Festival of Booths in Jerusalem. It is assumed that the festival has something to do with the promise of rain for the coming year; those who do not attend will not receive rain (v. 17).

The section in the Talmud dealing with Sukkot describes a ceremony that took place at the festival. On each of eight days a procession would go down to get water from the pool of Siloam. A golden pitcher was filled with water, carried to the temple and emptied out onto the altar. The Talmud associates all of this with the prophetic word in Isa. 12:3, "With joy you will draw water from the wells of salvation" (*The Babylonian Talmud, Seder Mo<sup>c</sup>ed*: Sukkah, trans. Israel W. Slotki [London: Soncino Press, 1938], 226–27).

In the context of this feast where water played such an important part, Jesus had something to say to those who were thirsty. In this setting of celebration and joy, Jesus cries out and makes an astounding claim. If you are really thirsty, he says, "come to me" (v. 37).

Here Jesus pits himself against the best that the religion of his day had to offer. Water symbolism abounded at this festival, with pitchers of water being carried to the temple each day, with the prophetic word about drawing water from the wells of salvation, and with the pouring out of the water symbolizing the hope for rain.

Now if you really want your "thirst" quenched, says Jesus, "come to me." He had said something similar to a woman of Samaria who was so unnerved by her encounter with him that she forgot her water jug at the well (John 4:7-30).

The translation of John 7:38 has long been debated. Does Jesus mean to say that "Out of the believer's heart shall flow rivers of living water" (NRSV) or rather "From within him [Jesus] shall flow rivers of living water?" The former seems to fit the context better, which then speaks about believers as channels for bringing the message of eternal life to others.

What Scripture passages was Jesus alluding to here? The answer is not clear, although a number of texts come to mind, including those that speak about life-giving water from the rock in the desert (Exod. 17:1-6) or the flowing of waters from the temple in God's kingdom (Ezek. 47:1-11).

The gift of "living water," says Jesus, refers to the pouring out of the Spirit, which would come after his death and resurrection (John 20:22). For John, this outpouring of the Spirit comes on the evening of Easter Day, and this account is sometimes called "John's Pentecost story." For Luke, the pouring out of the Spirit came later, at Pentecost. It is best to recognize that we have two conflicting memories about the date of this event. What both accounts agree on, however, is that after the resurrection, the disciples received the gift of the Holy Spirit.

The point of this text for preaching would seem to be as follows: Jesus pits himself against the best that religion up to his time had to offer. In the midst of the celebrating and rejoicing at this annual Jewish party, in the midst of recalling God's guidance in the wilderness and hoping for God's continued blessings of rain and crops in the future, Jesus puts it simply: If you really thirst, if you really long for that which can give you what you long for and hope for, come to me. Come to me and discover that the real life in this party is to be found in me. Because I am the way, the truth, and the life (14:6).